THIS IS
PERFECT

What to do when your
best falls short

NATHAN METZ

For my friends.

CHAPTERS

INTRODUCTION

Acts 16. Paul and Silas are in prison. Earlier that day they cast out a demon in a woman who had been using its evil power to tell fortunes. Of course, the fortune-telling power had been bringing her and her friends a nice little paycheck, so when Paul and Silas cast out the demon, those who were profiting became upset. After seeing their money source dry up, they went to authorities.

In prison, at about midnight, while Paul and Silas were singing hymns, an earthquake hit the cellblock, freeing all of the prisoners. With all of those inmates on the loose, the jail keeper thought he was ruined and decided to commit suicide. However, before he fell on his sword, Paul shouted to him that none of the prisoners were escaping. They were all there. The jail keeper fell before Paul and Silas and asked a very strange question: "What must I do to be saved?"

I have to admit something. Even though I'm pointing my finger at the jail keeper, I've asked the very same question. In fact, I would guess you have too because it's something we commonly consider when we go through anything like the jail keeper experienced. When we see the forces of God in front of us, we realize that we are at a point of decision.

The first leading steps of my faith came in the form of the jail keeper's loaded question: "What must I do to be saved?"

Admittedly, the question may not seem so strange at first glance, but let's think about it for a minute. What must I *do*? I smirk at the question now because it seems ridiculous. I think about the times I wondered what I should do, as if there was something I could *actually* do that might earn something. It's strange. We are lost in sin and weakness, and completely helpless to save ourselves. Yet we look to God, asking Him how we can help.

The absurdity is seen when we hold it up to the light of salvation and the life therein. These are free gifts because they were paid for by the One who had the power to do so. So what can we do? Nothing. Well, not nothing. We can believe in Him and love Him but nothing more. That's what Paul said in response to the jail keeper: "Believe in the Lord Jesus and you will be saved."

This book isn't about salvation though. Not really. It's about doing. It's about the strange question: "What must I do?" I found it wasn't just a question I asked only in regard to my salvation. It was a question I just kept asking and asking, sort of like a declaration of self-dependence and pride. I saw my desire for independence and my craving for self-reliance, and I expected both to bring power and authority to me. I wanted to take responsibility

3

for my religion. It wasn't actually about faith or relationship or love. It was about earning the right to live forever and avoiding punishment by being good enough and right enough.

What must we do? The question is far too often the ground floor of Christian teaching. Christians want to know how their lives are supposed to change. Our attempt to figure it out often comes in the form of behavioral questions. What do I do? What do I *not* do? How do I act? What do I wear and say? What should I spend my time on? How do I pray? What kinds of things should Christians be good at? We don't always ask these questions out loud. Sometimes we just think about them or use them as a barometer to judge those around us.

Usually this questioning comes from a good place, though. We all want to be the best we can be. We want to be perfect Christians and perfect spouses and perfect parents. We want to be a part of the perfect church and score the perfect dream job, all on the way to a perfect ending. The pressure is immense.

In this book we will work through the roots of this "what must we do" question on our way to a balanced response. If we do everything exactly right, are we guaranteed perfection? Is perfection even possible, or is it a word beyond humanity that just teases us in our floundering efforts? These are the questions I asked for years, questions which have ultimately formed the motivation for this book. They aren't without answer, but they do require some effort. Join me in asking God: What must we do?

CHAPTER ONE

THE PERFECT PROBLEM

Every book needs a problem to (hopefully) solve. This book finds its problem in holiness. Of course, holiness is not a problem in and of itself, but–in my case (and maybe yours too), it became one. I take quite seriously the problem of how I've understood the holiness message and attempted to apply it to my life. The "be holy" mandate from 1 Peter has towered over me like a tombstone for years-: "But just as he who called you is holy, so be holy in all you do; for it is written: 'Be holy, because I am holy.'[1]" I didn't get it. The language was too heavy. I was overwhelmed by the idea of having to be... that! I can't even say the word. It's too much. It's...well, it's PERFECT.

I first came to hear about 'Christian Perfection' through whispers and quick mentions in sermons here and there throughout my childhood. At that age, I didn't think much of its implications. I mean, there was a lot of that sort of vocabulary. Holiness. Perfection. Sanctification. It's high and lofty and so...Godly. To an optimistic little kid, it felt like a nice goal. Perfection...

Let me pause and explain something about myself. I was the first of three boys in the home of a pastor. My father led several churches during my childhood and our parents loved us well. To be perfectly clear, the church didn't burn me or let me down, No, my problem came before all that. I'm a first-born.

---

[1] 1 Peter 1:15-16

I suspect I might have done better if I was born second or even third. The pressure of being first was a blessing and a curse. I was always the first to grow up and move into the next stage of life. Big boy freedoms were mine first. My little brothers looked on in childish jealousy while I stomped around with pride because I was the only one allowed to do whatever. Unfortunately, I was also the first in line to walk into the unforeseen spider webs waiting for the face of a first-born, a leader's face, *my* face. My brothers could say, "Okay thanks for the heads-up, we'll not do it like that."

In my adult life, I've learned it's not just me. It's the way many first-born kids are. We like to lead. Sometimes that's a good thing, sometimes it's not. We like our ideas to be best. We tend to be the most competitive and struggle with losing (since we usually beat our younger siblings at everything). Most of all, we love being right and pleasing our parents in hopes of being their favorite.

As a child those behaviors were cute. I would draw the best picture or sing the song with the least amount of missed notes and mistaken lyrics. I would make up impossible games with my brothers and change the rules to make sure I always won. I guess that part wasn't quite as cute. Anyway, as I grew, my craving for perfection became an overwhelming problem. I couldn't respond well when my thoughts or ideas weren't exactly right. I wanted victory over the challenges life gave me, but if they were too difficult or I was intimated I would give up and say, "Well, I didn't want to do that anyway." I couldn't stand the thought of trying to the end and losing so I just quit early.

As a young man the emphasis on perfection entered into my understanding of how Christianity worked. It was all black and white to me. Simply put, either the matter was right or it was flat wrong. Then it went further. Right had to be the *most* excellent right. I couldn't just settle for soft applause from gracious spectators. I needed my right to be so right that it was praised and recognized as the *most* right. Surely there was a 'perfect', and I wanted to figure out what it was and live inside its glory.

I'm admitting some issues here to make a point. If I'm going to say something about holiness and Christian Perfection I need to be fair about my voice. I'm a perfectionist who had a problem with perfection. Big surprise.

I would love to just leave the whole thing at the statement: "a perfectionist had a problem with perfection." In fact, I almost did. But six or seven years ago I began the journey out of the whole mess, and it would have brought me comfort to find out the message was actually true, that I just didn't handle it well. Me. Just me. The problem was this: I wasn't alone.

The weight of perfection stands on the chest of many. In fact, it's not even just something we deal with in our little corner of the neighborhood. The burden of perfect living stretches through the whole of our

American history and culture[2], impacting the way we set our goals, parent our children, and reflect on the value of the life we have lived.

For many, it might seem odd to even refer to 'perfection' as a burden. Isn't perfection the gorgeous pinnacle of human achievement?

I have three daughters and a son. They are 10, 8, 7 and 3. The three-year-old is Ruby. She is the best daughter of all the three-year-old daughters in the world. I'm biased. If Ruby brings a coloring to me, like she did earlier today, I will smile and hug her and tell her it's perfect. Why? It *is* perfect. Do I mean her drawing is a flawless, one of a kind, world-class work of art? No. It's a scribbly, lopsided man with a big head on a torn piece of construction paper. I love it. It's from a right heart, and the expression it was intended to show hit the nail

---

[2] In 1949, H.L Mencken wrote this jab at our history of painful thinking: "Puritanism is the haunting fear that someone, somewhere may be happy. (Mencken)"

on the head. She wanted me to see that she loves me, and I feel her love. So, it's perfect.

For some, this definition of 'perfect' is old news. For others, it's revolutionary. Consider the change of tonality and purpose behind those Biblical mandates[3] putting words on us like excellence[4], perfect[5], and holy. If, for years, you have connected those words to some invisible and undefined standard, then I can assume you are just as exhausted as I was. The mind whirls around with unanswerable questions like:

What is excellence?

How much or how far is it?

How many errors are allowed?

What is perfect?

Can my perfect actually be perfect?

What is holy?

When is my holy actually holy enough?

---

[3] Mt 5:48, Phil 3:12, Col 1:28, James 1:4, Hebrews 12:14
[4] Phil 4:8
[5] 2 Corinthians 7:1

Aren't those thoughts torturous? It's a terribly painful place to live, yet many Christians find themselves exactly there. We do our best to wear a convincing smile and keep church relationships in tact. Yet, while others seem to be singing with joy, deep down we question whether we are clean enough, right enough, good enough, excellent, perfect, or holy. We measure ourselves against the people around us and look for ways to feel good about our Christianity. In this way, holiness becomes a contest of churchy behavior. The filling of the Holy Spirit is replaced by the mimicry of whatever person we think acts the most like a good Christian. This reduces what we know of holiness to performance and places an awful weight on our hearts. This problem that I've just described is common (you're not alone) and it's nothing close to holiness.

True holiness brings joy. True holiness brings peace. True holiness brings ambition, purpose and passion. If holiness has become a burdensome intimidation then it's not holiness any more. It's time to make a change.

Together, let's travel in the chapters to follow as we search for God's intentions in holiness and the true meaning of Christian Perfection. It's a journey to wide open spaces, deep breaths of fresh air, and a feeling of freedom unlike anything this side of eternity could ever offer.

CHAPTER TWO

GETTING IT RIGHT

Every third Sunday of the month I preach for Rev. James Ouma at our local church in a part of town called Kisugu. I live in Africa, by the way. We are missionaries in Uganda, a little country right in the middle of the continent. Rev. James is a close friend of mine who is currently working on his doctorate, so he's a pretty busy guy. As a Kenyan missionary to Uganda, he is currently the head pastor at our church, I love working with him.

Before he introduced me as the speaker this morning, he needed to take care of some business. Apparently there have been some members of the church who have requested the teaching lighten up and relax a bit. They thought the holiness stuff had been good but maybe a little too heavy. They wanted the preaching to include lighter topics and requested that the preachers "relax." In response, Rev. James gave them a loving but firm "no." He explained that the holiness message might be heavy at times but it mustn't be compromised.

As I sat in my seat holding my sermon notes, I thought, "Isn't that strange. I am on the other side of the planet and even here the message of holiness feels 'heavy'." The fact that Africans respond in a similar way as Americans is not surprising at all. We're all people. What surprises me is the vastness of this crippling thinking on such an important Biblical topic.

It seems we need a better definition. We need to correctly adjust our perspective of these important words and ideas. Here's the truth: nothing is lighter on the human spirit than holiness. When God calls us into Himself, He calls us into peace and wholeness. Out of the darkness we are called into the light. Evil attacks the human spirit without mercy as it seeks to devastate and destroy. Sin ravages humanity and drains us into dryness. Holiness is the cure.

We only feel the weight of holiness when we incorrectly assign ourselves the responsibility to make it happen. Those words "be holy" are not instructions for human *action* so much as they are instruction for human *reception*. We don't make it, we receive it. We do not create holiness anywhere, especially not in ourselves. Paul speaks quite directly to this point in his letter to the Galatians: "Are you so foolish? Having begun by the Spirit, are you now being perfected by the flesh?"[6] Only God is holy and all holiness comes from Him[7].

---

[6] Galatians 3:3
[7] 1 Samuel 2:2

And what about perfection? What do we mean by that word? Occasionally, I wake up and leave the pastorish/missionaryish clothes in the closet in favor of old jeans, a stained t-shirt, and my orange shoes (which have seen better days). On those mornings I go into the garage, look at the lumber I have available, and dive into some sort of building project. Most of the time my projects come out nicely but not always. Don't ask my wife what she thinks of the doghouse I built a few months ago…or the sawdust.

Kevin, a buddy of mine who is ten years younger than me, also enjoys woodworking. His age makes him the perfect candidate to grip a piece of sandpaper and finish up one of our projects, saving me from a sore back the next day. I'm usually ready for the work to be done before he is. By the time the sun goes down, I'm tired, and we still have tools to put away, yet there he is, still sanding. Even past dark he is looking the thing over to make sure it's just right. I don't know how he sands in the dark but when morning comes around whatever project we conquered looks pretty good. I think it looks good because of his devotion toward the *perfection* of the project. Even when a table or a bed or whatever we are building seemed finished, Kevin still had *perfecting* work to add. First, he used a heavyweight sandpaper to take remove any bumps, stubborn grains, and knots in the wood. As he smooths it, he changes to a lighter grit paper to eliminate even smaller marks and scratches. Finally, he uses his last smoothing paper and says, "I'm nearly done. I'm just making some final *perfections*."

Using Kevin's approach to woodworking, we see the truth of how perfection becomes a process of finishing rather than an arrival at the finish line. In fact, when Kevin is done, he never says, "Tada! It's perfect!" His perfecting work was about improvement and progress. By that example we see how God's perfections take a while, and they never end. By His *perfecting* hand, also called 'perfecting grace', we are taken deeper and deeper into the infinite depths of His glory.

So how do we feel about *that* definition of the word? Better? Perfection is not the static, finalized standard by which we are to live, but instead the method by which we grow and mature[8]. If you think about it, the word perfect can be used the same way. Kevin was nearly finished but still wanted to 'perfect' his project. 1 Peter 5:10 uses the word that way saying that God "will Himself perfect, confirm, strengthen and establish you."[9] He will continue to perfect it until it's perfect. It's a process.

I keep using this term "perfect" but I wonder if there might be some readers who aren't on the same wavelength yet. It's not just about the current definition of the term or the Biblical meaning, it's about the history of the thing. Where did it come from? The whole phrase is this: Christian Perfection. It's old. I'm going to guess maybe not all of us are completely familiar with the term Christian

---

[8] Hebrews 6:1 is a great example to this point. Half of our translations use some form of the word "perfect" while the other half use some form of the word "mature".

[9] 1 Peter 5:10

Perfection, so let's dive into some background on where the phrase comes from and how it has impacted the church.

CHAPTER THREE

JOHN & CHARLES

John was born in 1703, four years before his big brother Charles. Their father and grandfather were both musicians, a talent passed to Charles who would go on to write over 6,000 hymns in his lifetime. They were well-educated, Godly young men who frequently worked together in ministry throughout their lives.

John Wesley became a famous orator, pastor, and church leader. He was fascinated with the more personal aspects of the Christian faith such as emotions, heart change, thought life, etc. He spent much time and effort studying the Bible in it's teaching on sanctification and holy living. He became convinced that the Church had not been teaching the Biblical message of holiness in fullness with practical relevance. Kenneth Collins wrote that Wesley "underscored the importance of being not a nominal Christian, conformed in outward form only, but of being a real Christian, one who by the grace of God has been transformed in holiness and in power."[10] Charles had previously founded the Holy Club at Oxford, a small social group committed to developing holy living in its members. Later, John would lead the group and continue forming his thoughts on sanctification and the power of God to bring victory over sin.

In 1766, at the age of 63, John published a book that became a Christian classic titled "A

---

[10] Kenneth Collins, *The Scripture Way of Salvation*, (Abingdon Press, 1997), p. 152

Plain Account of Christian Perfection." He opened his book with a statement of purpose, aiming "to give a plain and distinct account of the steps by which (he) was led, during a course of many years, to embrace the doctrine of Christian perfection."[11] Wesley went on to explain what he meant by Christian Perfection (and what he did *not* mean). He discussed possible dangers and oppositions, and responded to common questions. Midway through his book he described the 'perfect man' as "sanctified throughout, even to have a heart so all-flaming with the love of God as continually to offer up every thought, word and work as a spiritual sacrifice, acceptable to God through Christ. In every thought of our hearts, in every word of our tongues, in every work of our hands, to show forth his praise, who hath called us out of darkness into His marvelous light."[12] Pretty good stuff, eh? If

---

[11] John Wesley, *A Plain Account of Christian Perfection (Beacon Hill Press, 1966), p. 9*

[12] John Wesley, *A Plain Account of Christian Perfection (Beacon Hill Press, 1966), p. 37*

you like those words, you aren't alone. His ideas exploded.

After his death in 1792, John Wesley's teaching continued to grow in popularity and by the mid-1800's, a holiness movement had begun. Born from this movement were the Methodists, named for the 'method' originating back in the Holy Club. Periodicals like the 'Guide to Christian Perfection' and the 'Beauty of Holiness' helped spread the teaching and unify those who agreed. Many books, positions, and arguments, both for and against, were written and published. Some denominations were formed, some split, and others merged.

Much of the splitting and merging was connected to the doctrine of Christian Perfection, its development and impact on those for or against. The doctrine underwent significant scrutiny and a universally accepted definition was hard to come by. During the next hundred years many mergers would occur like the International Holiness Church with the Pilgrim Church in 1917 and The Holiness

Church with the Pilgrim Holiness Church in 1946. All of these mergers culminated with the most recent merger of the Pilgrim Holiness Church and The Wesleyan Methodist Church of America in 1968.[13] This merger created The Wesleyan Church, the denomination I was born into and the one I belong to today.

While historical background information gives us a glimpse into the story behind Christian Perfection, there are many terms and phrases that refer to the same thing. W. T. Purkiser explained how the "crisis in the individual spiritual life is known as holiness, entire sanctification, the fullness of the Spirit, evangelical perfection, Christian perfection, perfect love, heart purity, the rest of faith, the spiritual man, full salvation, circumcision of the heart, the fullness of the blessing of Christ, and the baptism with the Spirit."[14] So it's not really a new concept at all. Unfortunately though, it hasn't been updated much either. We've

---

[13] Lee Haines and Paul Thomas, *An Outline History of The Wesleyan Church*, (Wesleyan Publishing House, 2005), p. 59

[14] W. T. Purkiser, *Exploring Christian Holiness, Vol. 1: The Biblical Foundations*, (Beacon Hill Press of Kansas City, 1983)

stopped using some of the older language (like 'perfection'), but we haven't really replaced it with anything new. In fact, most of the current leaders in our denomination agree the holiness movement is over. While many denominations and organizations were actually established during the movement and are still around today, the movement itself has been reduced to a few dates and notes in the history books.

So now what do we do? Hopefully from this brief jaunt through history we have a better understanding of where these feelings about church expectation and religious behavior originated. For those who felt church was rigid, rule based, works oriented, and harsh, I understand. So did I. It helped me quite a bit to see some history behind how we managed to arrive here. It wasn't that they were mean people. Although their hearts were in the right place, followers were living inside a dried up method. The damage occurred when those old methods and lifestyle practices became an end in themselves rather than an expression of an inner change. Generations failed to pass on the heart of the matter, that God's love radically changes us. Somehow the social pressure of a holy appearance became an overwhelming force. John Wesley, noticing the problem early on, commented, "The most prevailing fault among the Methodists is to be *too outward* in religion. We are continually forgetting that the kingdom of God is *within* us."[15] The outward religion grew into a legalistic and socially oppressive system, pushing droves of young people like me out of the church.

The challenge now is to find our balance again. Obviously, it's not wise to just toss the whole thing out even if the wrongs of the past brought pain. Holiness is Biblical. Even if our flawed history within the teaching caused damage, I'm still drawn to Wesley's understanding of what a Christian life should look like. As intimidating as it is, even with the pain it's caused, I'm attracted to it. Perhaps what we need is to revisit the main point.

---

[15] Kenneth Collins, *The Scripture Way of Salvation*, (Abingdon Press, 1997), p. 164

Perhaps with a balanced Biblical definition of holiness we can use a word like 'perfect[16]' in every day life and feel good about it. If that's true, if perfect is possible, count me in.

---

[16] Look at how Hebrews 10:14 uses the word: "For by that one offering he forever made perfect those who are being made holy." Perfect is a description of the *current* condition of those who are in the *process* of being made holy. In other words, if the ongoing work of holiness is currently happening to you then you are perfect.

CHAPTER FOUR

WHAT I BELIEVE

B efore we jump into the practical let me finish up these initial thoughts with some work in definitions. I need to be up front and just say what I *do* believe. So far I've uncovered my personal struggles, disagreements, and how everything seemed to flip upside down. So let's put things back into balance by placing my own neck on the chopping block.

The real point of this particular chapter is to introduce some terminology and various definitions or connotations behind the words we use. A wrong or confused understanding of a word welcomes a losing battle[17]. To avoid those battles, I want to make sure we are all on the same page before we go much farther.

For the sake of avoiding a generic textbook list of terms, let's create a fictional character and call him George. In this chapter, George will begin as someone who does not believe in Jesus Christ as his Savior. In fact, George doesn't believe in God at all. However, by the end, George will be saved and grow in Christian Perfection and help me to put into words the belief I now hold on the subject.

George is not a Christian. He grew up in a home in which religion was rarely spoken and church was not a part of the family's weekly events. He knew a little bit about what went on at church from his limited

---

[17] Commenting on the impact of Wesley's inconsistencies in his terminology, Peter's wrote "It is quite possible to quote Wesley at length against Wesley." *Christian Perfection and American Methodism*, p. 64

experience with Christmas, Easter, and the occasional special community event or whatever else happened to bring his family into their local sanctuary. As an adult, George avoided conversations about God because he didn't care to even defend his position. Privately, he would tell you that he didn't believe in God because it didn't make any sense. In fact, he sometimes wondered whether God was just something people made up because they were lonely or couldn't handle life.

George's life was actually pretty decent. He had a job he loved, a wife he loved, kids he loved and a few admirable goals for the future. As a result, he didn't feel he needed much.

Unfortunately, as is common, George experienced a tragedy. I'm not going to say what it is because it doesn't really matter. (This story is made up anyway.) The point is: his life was changed which caused him to take another look at his belief system *and his ability to control his existence.*

During his time of self-introspection, George allowed for the slight possibility that God might exist and that he, George, might even be helped by having a relationship with God. This moment of recognition is important. It's not salvation. It's comes before anything contractual or formally binding. It's a curiosity and interest that paves the way for future decision-making. This event often occurs around experiences that bring us face-to-face with our mortality. Funerals, serious accidents, threatening illnesses, surgery and a host of other potentially deadly situations tend to show us our human weakness, frailty and inability to save ourselves or protect our future. For this reason, in these moments we often search for the presence of God. Even those who do not call themselves "Christian" tend to think about God and ask questions. Sometimes these thoughts take root and grow into a vibrant faith in Jesus Christ. Not always. Sometimes.

Over the next couple of weeks George frequently considered these thoughts. When he saw religion in a news article or a book he would flip through the pages with curiosity. He wasn't making any major decisions, but his eyes were opening.

On his way home from work one night he drove past the local church, just like he had every night for years. On this particular night however, he noticed the lights were on and the doors were open. Feeling compelled to stop, George pulled into the lot and parked his car.

George's moment of compulsion is the work of the Holy Spirit. God the Holy Spirit woos and tugs on the hearts of humanity, pulling us in the direction of the Father through the Work of the Son.[18]

---

[18] John 16:12-15

George stepped out of his car and wandered toward the doors of the church. He started feeling emotional and wasn't sure why. Actually, he felt silly about being emotional and quickly cleaned up his eyes with his wrist. By that time, he was standing in the foyer. He didn't see anyone so he decided to sit down in the back of the sanctuary. A moment later, an older man came through a door on the opposite side of the room. He was pulling a sweeper and whistling. George began crying again but still didn't know what he was feeling.

George's emotional response is also a work of the Holy Spirit called *conviction*. Too often Christians assume the weighted responsibility of assigning conviction of sin to everyone around them, making sure those people know what they did wrong. How tragic! The Bible makes it clear that it is the work of the Holy Spirit to convict.[19] Sure, the Holy Spirit might

---

[19] John 16:8-11

use us as a part of the communication in the work, but we should never elevate ourselves to such a task without being clearly called and equipped to do so.

As George sat under the dimmed lighting in the old church, eyes shining with tears, the man with the sweeper made his way over to the outlet on the wall. After plugging in his cord, he stood up and noticed the emotional stranger in the back of the otherwise empty sanctuary.

"Hello!," he said quite happily.

George waved shyly even though he wasn't really a shy person. He just wasn't confident how to behave in the moment. Half of him wanted to stand up and go home. The other half felt like his jeans were nailed to the wooden pew.

The old man put the sweeper to the side and hobbled his way down the isle. He took a seat in the pew just in front of George and offered him his hand. George shook it.

"I'm Peter."

"George"

"Nice to meet you."

Peter paused for a moment before speaking again.

"Hey, if you don't mind me askin', are you okay? I haven't seen you here before have I? Everything alright?"

Over the next few minutes Peter would talk about whatever George had on his mind. Sometimes George would say something really off base and other times he seemed to be moving in a good direction. Throughout the talk, Peter patiently allowed George to speak and share what was on his heart.

In that conversation, George brought up the topic of God. He told Peter how his thoughts had recently changed, and he wasn't sure what to do about it. Peter shared some of his own story of how he went through something quite similar years ago. George appreciated having someone to share this with, especially since they had some similar thoughts and ideas.

Eventually George fell silent and looked down at his hands that lay still on his knees. Peter consoled him by assuring George that life could be different. He explained what faith meant and who Jesus really was and what it meant to believe in Him. George listened cautiously but with interest.

Peter finished his mini-sermon saying, "You can make a decision tonight if you think you're ready. But, you know, this isn't the kind of thing to do on a whim. I'm not pushing you."

"I know. I've been thinking about this for a long time, though. I want to move forward."

"Well that's great!"

"What do I do?"

Peter helped George through a prayer of personal repentance and receiving of forgiveness. They were slow and deliberate, waiting on the Spirit and not pushing through to take anything quickly with a series of words or phrases. In the end, Peter put his hand on George's shoulder and asked, "Has God spoken to you?" With a slight quiver in his voice George replied, "yes."

I believe three things happened, all at the same time, all within George's moment of salvation.

Firstly, George has been justified. Justification is the making right of the relationship between God and man[20]. In justification, the penalty for sin is removed, and the person can be called 'righteous.' Justification only occurs when true repentance is met with God's forgiveness. His forgiveness is full and firm, causing the forgiven person to receive the benefits of a right relationship with

---

[20] 2 Corinthians 5:21

God. Romans 5:1 says, "Being justified by faith, we have peace with God through our Lord Jesus Christ."

Secondly, George has been regenerated. Regeneration is another word for rebirth, which is where we gain the term 'born again.' In regeneration, the Holy Spirit imparts the spiritual life in place of what was dead prior to salvation.[21] A regenerated person is awakened to the capabilities, characteristics, and functions of the new nature in Christ.

Finally, George has begun the process of sanctification. You see, once the moment in church is over, George goes home. His family is unchanged, his work is unchanged and even within his own person, his habits and routines are unchanged. George still has a long way to go! The process of "going", the continued change and growth into the image of Christ is called sanctification.[22]

---

[21] John 3:5-8

[22] Philippians 3

Over the next years of his life, George continued an upward movement in the faith, maturing in Christ and growing in character and discipline. George was being made into a new man! Those who knew George from the beginning could hardly recognize him. He looked the same and sounded the same, but his character changed every day. Humble, compassionate and joyful became common words used to describe him, a certain change from his past reputation.

George knew he was changing, too. Since that night, years ago, in the quiet little church with Peter the custodian, George had been moving forward. The regeneration that took place in him was thorough and lasting. Through discipleship and the consistent love and care of those elder Christians around him, George matured in Christ. The Holy Spirit continued to grow him and shape him day by day.

Eventually, George started to recognize just how deeply his heart had been changed. His pursuit of God had been absolute for years and his disciplined focus on love and worship were a thing of beauty. Now, after all the growth, he felt a new movement, a new touch to his soul. He prayed again saying, "God, if there is anything in me that is bent away from you, anything selfish, anything prideful, convict me now and cleanse me fully!" The Holy Spirit replied with a comforting presence, giving George an assurance that his heart was truly aimed at God, without competition or wrong motivation.

The next day George felt strange. On one hand, he felt a new sense of purity and intimacy with God. On the other hand, he still felt a battle against temptation, evil, and the pressures of a fallen world, but they were much less influential. He was not sinless, but he was freed from the draw to intentional sinful behavior. He was not excellent in thought or action or even in wisdom, yet he knew something was different, although he wasn't sure what to call it.

At this point in the story, George is perfect. Biblically speaking, George has fulfilled the instruction of Jesus to be perfect. You know the statement in Matthew 5:48 where Jesus gives that command we didn't like: "Be perfect, therefore, as your heavenly Father is perfect." Well, George did it!

The question we must ask though is this: Be perfect in *what*? Conduct? Performance? Outward Christian living? Or something else? Well, look at the context in which these words were spoken. In the middle of a sermon Jesus says a few things about love. He raises the bar on what most were saying and told the people that we don't just love those who love us, we are to love our enemies, too. As followers of His teaching we often respond saying, "What kind of a heart could possibly love an enemy!"[23] What kind of a heart? The perfect heart. Jesus

---

[23] Mt 5:44

taught us to aim our hearts at God without compromise or ulterior motives. We are to desire God above all things. We make our hearts' desire for Him an unchallenged, dominant and driving force behind every movement of life. This is perfect!

George was perfect because he had nothing in his heart but love for God. All George wanted was to love God fully and with the best and biggest love he could. If, in that loving endeavor, George messed up or made a mistake, even a big one, his heart was still perfect. A human with a perfect heart is still a human.[24] Perfect ain't always perfect[25].

A perfect human heart, even in its weakness, will not always be able to see or identify the hidden impulses.[26] If it could, the perfect heart would seek to destroy them and anything else that fell short of perfection. It's

---

[24] Ephesians 4:11-16
[25] During the development of this book I asked one of my daughters friends what she thought of the cover. At eleven years old she said, "It says it's perfect but it isn't". I laughed and said, "great answer!"
[26] Daniel 2:22

possible to have a perfect heart, aimed right at God, with a buried desire or motivation that is yet to be revealed[27].

George will mess up in the future, but not because his perfectly oriented heart has twisted around itself. George is a human. Even his heart, righteous and pure, cannot see to the depths of his spirit. Only the Holy Spirit of God can see down there!

Consider King David, the man after God's own heart[28]. His heart was aimed in the perfect direction, but he too fell into sin. Is the heart an excuse for sin? Could David have looked at the temptation and sin in front of him and claimed his innocence? Absolutely not! It makes no sense to talk about this perfect heart if we are going to make it an excuse to sin. The perfect heart hates sin! Even the perfect heart cannot see sinful motivations and desires and must therefore

---

[27] Romans 7:14-25
[28] Acts 13:22

continue in dependence on God for wisdom and guidance.

Dr. John Oswalt makes the point very clear in his influential book on holiness "Called to Be Holy." He writes:

> *Psalm 51 speaks of something of the shock that came to David when he saw the full horror of what he had done with Bathsheba and Uriah. So he pleads for a cleansing which will be deeper than anything he has known before. Something of the same sort appears at the end of Psalm 19 and again at the end of Psalm 139. Thus, a way that is perfect in the sense that it is marked by unblemished devotion and obedience may not be a way that is necessarily perfect in performance. There may be a hundred and one things that prevent us from performing perfectly, but on the basis of these biblical statements, it is entirely possible for a human to walk perfectly before God. In fact, the Bible says that this is the minimum*

requirement for those who would serve God.[29]

Christian Perfection, holiness, sanctification, excellence, and whatever other 'standard of Christianity' words or phrases we want to throw in the mix, address motivation, the heart, the intention, and the desire. To some, this might sound weak, like we are lowering the bar or settling for something less. It's not weak, though. It's just right. It's the very language used to describe King Asa in 1 Kings 15:14, "Although he did not remove the high places, Asa's heart was fully committed to the Lord all his life." Asa was imperfect in his outward performance but perfect in inward intentions.

Put simply, perfection by any other definition but motivation makes no sense at all. Only God is perfect in performance. Only God is perfect in outcomes. Of course God would not create finite, limited beings and

---

[29] John Oswalt, *Called to Be Holy*, (Francis Asbury Press, 1999)

know them in their weakness and then call them to something completely unreachable. Rather, He calls us to be perfect in our hopes, wants, desires, motivations, goals, etc. Just like He is perfect in His motivation, He wants perfection in our motivation. In the words of Paul, Christian living becomes "instinctive" and is "written on our hearts" so that our "conscience and thoughts either accuse us or tell us we are doing right.[30]

Take a moment to read Psalm 139. It's a beautiful poem about the intimate relationship we can have with God. He knows us full well! He is behind and before. He knit us together in the womb! God loves us intimately! At the end of the poem, the writer reveals the pure love in the matter. When a person loves God deeply, like the author of this poem, they talk to Him like this: "Search me, O God, and know my heart; test me and know my anxious thoughts. Point out anything in me that offends you, and lead me along the path of everlasting life." Try memorizing that verse

---

[30] Romans 2:14-15

and speaking it out loud to start the day and/or end the day. Christian perfection isn't about gritting your teeth and trying again and again to get the rules exactly right day after day. The psalmist didn't write "know my performance" but rather "know my heart".

In order to properly understand Christian Perfection, there must be a right, healthy, balanced idea of the concept which will in turn allow us to apply its principles to our positions and places in life. In other words, if we are going to do this then we need to start talking about some examples. It's time to be practical. How can we be perfect? Let's talk about it.

THE PERFECT CHRISTIAN

One: I am 100% sure I am a Christian. Two: I have no idea when I became a Christian. Those two statements (which are true about me) might seem like a stark contrast to all the testimonies we've heard where some have remembered fondly the very date and time of their moment of salvation. However, the rest of us, quietly, have no idea. We can't name a time or even a place. Our commitment to the faith wasn't marked as an instantaneous situation. Ours was slow and tedious. While they were marking the calendar we were gritting our teeth and holding on for dear life! It might have moved faster had it not been for all those times we got distracted, confused or stopped completely with discouragement.

My journey toward the faith I have now, the "100% sure" kind, took around five years which were marked by individual moments where a deepening of sincerity and faith occurred in various degrees. Sometimes it was very emotional. Sometimes it was almost completely intellectual. Sometimes it was a confirmation. Sometimes it was a brand new revelation. No matter what the moment looked like or how I describe it today, the result was always the same: nearer Lord to thee.

Whatever perfection existed in my heart served to usher me deeper into the holiness of God, deeper into His glory. It wasn't because I had achieved anything at the time. I hadn't. The forward movement into a deeper relationship with God came as His response to my heart's desire. I wanted Him. "For I am confident of this very thing, that He who began a good work in you will perfect it until the day of Christ Jesus."[31]

As previously confessed, it wasn't always this way for me. For years I had the whole thing upside down. When I was in middle school I remember a teacher asking me what my goals were for the class. "Do you want to set a goal to get at least a B?" I was baffled. A *what*? Why would I set a goal to earn a B? I'll set the goal for an A and then deal with the disappointment of a B if such a strange and impossible thing could ever happen. I never understood why I should *try* for an easy B. Anyway, I landed a solid C.

My same mentality followed me into religion as a young adult. Essentially, I wanted to be a *perfect* Christian. I wanted the A.

I think most of us fit into one of two distinct categories, either we try for the A in Christianity and then wrestle with the results for years, or we try for the B and wrestle with

---

the results for years. Either way, we are working toward a grade. We are achieving. The perfect Christian isn't thinking about achievements.

The word 'Christian' means "follower of Christ." It would seem to make sense then that a perfect Christian is someone who "follows Christ perfectly" which is not necessarily true. Like most of us, the famed theologian Adam Clarke didn't like the word 'perfect' either. He once wrote that he would *gladly lay it by and employ a word more worthy, but there is none in our language."* John Peters commented on Clarke:

> *Taking the term as it stands, however, Clarke concludes that the perfect is that which fully answers the end for which it was created. And since man was created to love God "with all his heart, soul, mind and strength, and his neighbor as himself," he who does so is perfect.*[32]

[32] John L. Peters, *Christian Perfection and American Methodism*, (Abingdon Press, 1956)

Peter's nice, little summarizing statement at the end there explains the perfect Christian as one who does what a human being was designed to do: love God with heart, soul, mind, and strength, and love his neighbor as himself. There really is nothing more to add if we are only discussing the very center of the answer. I haven't elaborated or gone anywhere further than Scripture but our entire position, this whole doctrine, all these pages leading up to now stand on the one idea: love. In fact, in an old book "Perfect Love" which sits on my shelf as a fairly regular reference, J.A. Wood describes Christian Perfection as "the possession of pure love to God."[33] A perfect Christian is a person whose love for God is pure.

Whatever else is said about the life of a Christian being perfect must begin and end with a pure love for God[34]. Pure love refers to motivation, intention, dedication, and

---

[33] J.A. Wood, *Perfect Love*, (Beacon Hill Press, 1912), p. 20
[34] 1 Timothy 2:22 describe the Christian attributes as living "along with those who call on the Lord with a pure heart".

obedience. I can't speak for your motivation. You can't speak for mine, either. The same is true about intentions, dedication, and obedience. We could probably make some guesses but no man can see the heart of another. The state of my love sits fixed between two parties: myself and my God.

When we define a perfect Christian by describing the heart, we immediately remove external behaviors from our focus. We can't see it, touch it, smell it or hear it in another person. If it's a heart condition like motivation or dedication then it's internal. This attention on the internal situation has always been there[35]. It's not like we grow as Christians and mature to a certain point where suddenly God begins to consider the condition of our soul. From the beginning God has been more interested in the direction we are heading rather than the distance we have travelled or the effort we've put in. In a letter to Timothy

---

[35] Phil 1:15-19 refers to preachers who "do not have pure motives". Yet, even with wrong motives he says "the message of Christ is preached" and so he rejoices. Notice his attention to the inside condition and its impact on the outside expression.

about the work of ministry, Paul rooted his instruction with these words: "The goal of this command is love, which comes from a pure heart and a good conscience and a sincere faith."[36] God places motivation above accomplishment. He asks "why" before He asks "what." The thirteenth century German theologian Meister Eckhart wrote, "People should not worry as much about what they do but rather about what they are"[37 & 38]. Young Christians might feel as if God is always looking over their shoulders to see if they are sinning and when they are caught they imagine God in great drama asking them, "What have you done?" We should remember that God doesn't need the information. It's not as if He actually wonders about anything, hoping we are honest in telling Him *what* we have done so

---

[36] 1 Timothy 1:5

[37] Meister Eckhart, *Selected Writings, (Penguin UK, 1994)*

[38] He went on to write, "If they and their ways are good, then their deeds are radiant. If you are righteous, then what you do will also be righteous. We should not think that holiness is based on what we do but rather on what we are, for it is not our works which sanctify us but we who sanctified our works."

He has an accurate account. The point is not *what* we did but *why* we did it. In order to intentionally sin against God, the heart must first turn away from Him[39]. At the moment it turns away, the relationship is damaged, but redemption occurs at the will of God. Again, not because of *what* we did but *why* we did it.

Things work this way because God loves us. The statement "because God loves us" only matters because it is *God* who loves. If Joe or Amber or some other person you know loves you then great. I'm happy for you. But the love of a person is not the same as the love of God. No human love can do what God's love can do. If we believe God is who He says He is and does what He says He does then our whole vocabulary must be turned on it's head. The *why* comes before the *what* only because the love of God has power. God knows that if we return to His love, the *why* will be repaired and the *what* will follow.

---

[39] Deut 30:17

Rather than a constant response to a broken relationship, God desires to transform us into people who stop breaking the relationship in the first place. Pure love is not about the actions of the body but the direction of the heart. The body doesn't move contrary to the heart. Priorities impact our day, shape the decisions we make, and even determine the way we speak and move and sit and walk and shake a hand and eat. A changed heart is a changed person. God is not so weak to simply train us like dogs, working only toward the exterior self to demand behavior while tricking us with little treats and smacking us on the nose if we mess up. God moves into our lives with the power to touch the soul. He begins at the center, the heart, purifying our love for Him. The result of a pure love for Him is a changed person with changed behaviors; visible, external, social, and seen.

In the chapters to follow I can be even more practical in my approach because in this chapter I've laid a correct foundation. There is not one single action of a Christian that can be called anything close to perfect if it does not come from a heart of pure love for God. Even the most righteous acts are worth nothing if they come from a heart faced in the wrong direction.[40] However, even if the heart is perfect in direction, the Christian will screw up sometimes because we can't ever be the identical duplication of Jesus Christ. The whole "WWJD" thing is an impossible, impersonal mind game. We don't ask ourselves what Jesus *would* do as if he were some dead guy who we all agreed to mimic. We ask ourselves what Jesus *is* doing, actively, currently, in us and through us right now! Our pure love for God is the result of Christ's Work active in our lives today. A perfect Christian isn't the exactness of Jesus Christ but the whole-hearted, surrendered, and sanctified follower He calls.

If the direction of the heart is correct then the actions of the body will follow. The feet follow the heart. Aim the heart correctly, and the rest will fall in line.

---

[40] 1 Cor 13:1-3

What is the perfect Christian? The perfect Christian knows without a doubt there is not a single thread of any fiber in the body that intends, wants, or desires anything away from God. The perfect Christian responds to God's voice with a bent knee and a breaking heart, seeking to glorify the One in glory and worship the One who is worthy. The perfect Christian is agile in obedience, a sponge to conviction, and a soldier to service. To the knowledge of the perfect Christian, not one single thought has escaped the light nor a single image spared from the Lord. To the future of the perfect Christian, there is no day, year, hope, or dream that hasn't been abandoned to God and fastened to His will. To the heart of the perfect Christian, there is nothing greater, hotter or more dominating than the love for God spitting flames higher every day. Mistakes are met with prayer. Error is met with repentance. Every wrong action, lost word, misplaced deed, or misunderstanding is plunged into the blood of Christ with a Godly sorrow. Perfect Christians claim no reward of their own merit and no title to prove their worth. If a reward is mentioned they point to salvation. If a title is mentioned they proudly stand as "son" or "daughter" adopted into the family of the God they love. With all their *heart* they love their Lord. With all their *soul* they love their Lord. With all their *mind* they love their Lord. The perfect Christian is filled up by the love of God until it hits the brim and gushes over into the lives of those around them. Their neighbors speak of them as loving, kind, and full of peace and joy. When the topic turns to death, their topic turns to Christ for in Him death is defeated. This life, to a perfect Christian, is a whisper lost in the cheers and choirs of Heaven's eternal song.

How can you live this way? Love the Lord your God with all your heart, soul, mind, and strength. Love your neighbor as yourself.

CHAPTER SIX

THE PERFECT SPOUSE

I t's the classic love story: the perfect guy, the perfect girl, each desperately searching for the perfect love. They meet, smitten and entranced by the other. Her hair blows ever so softly in the wind while the star-crossed pair exchange flirtatious smiles and enticing glances all to the soundtrack of a heart pounding romance. Audiences are drawn into their perfect ending as we imagine ridiculous scenes about their happily-ever-after, totally void of all problems and worries, and constantly just gushing at the seams with lovey-dovey mush…hair still blowing the wind. I guess I'm not a romantic.

When the movie ends and it's back to reality for the rest of us, the snack bowls need to be taken into the kitchen and cleaned, and the dog needs to be let outside one last time. So dreamy.

I've thought about this movie genre before and wondered about our fascination with 'the perfect' spouse. It's interesting that these movies are never about *being* the perfect spouse, just *finding* one.

I got married a little over ten years ago. I'm 34 now; my wife is 32. Our marriage has changed and evolved just as we have individually changed and evolved. We fight. We hug. We find shared joys and laughter. In some ways you could say we fight through life together. In our spousal efforts there is not much to call perfect. We mess up all the time. Using what we've learned so far though, there is a different way of understanding perfect. We look at the intentions, the hopes and purposes of the marriage. To define the perfect spouse we should be asking a few questions. Why do we even get married? What should our marriages produce? Using the description of the perfect Christian, who is the perfect spouse?

The answers to these questions might seem like unreachable ideals. They certainly aren't easy but we should be careful not to point at God's designs and call them unreachable. Our faith in Him should cause us to reexamine how we consider the possibilities of this life. Remember, God does not create plans and call us to live them out if He knows there is no possibility of us doing so. If He says, "Do this" then He is also saying, "This is possible for you." Of course, it isn't possible on our own. God declares the plan and then tells us it's possible for us but only if we are walking in the Spirit, alive in Christ. It's possible because He makes it possible. With that in mind, know this: the perfect spouse is possible.

The perfect spouse is a spouse second to a much greater love affair. No matter how beautiful the bride or groom is on the wedding day, the perfect spouse has a deeper and stronger love tethered to another. From the day they met, the other love, the love for Christ, has been dominant. The marital love does not compete with God for first place. Priority is given to a time of intimacy and togetherness between the spouse and the Lord.

This first love is not one that distracts or diminishes from the marital love. In fact, because God is the Source of love, the marital love will then grow and be purified. No other comparable factor can multiply the love in a marriage more than the protected and prioritized love for Jesus Christ. No amount of romantic dates, vacations, cuddling, or flirting can increase the quality of love in a marriage like a relationship with God.

The husband will love his wife best when he loves Christ most. If the wife wants to love her husband fully, she should love her Lord firstly. The perfect spouse is a spouse second and a lover of Christ first. If the marriage is healthy, the spouses should encourage each other in the direction of Christ above any other. True love wants the best for the beloved. If we love our spouses perfectly, we will love them into the arms of Christ before our own. To borrow the words of Paul, "we want to present them to God, perfect in their relationship to Christ."[41] When held in Him, they are loved more fully than we could ever love them.

In their devotions we make an effort in the house to give them privacy and silence. In their struggles we point them to Christ and share in their seeking of Him. The perfect marriage is one where every motivation is focused on the worship of Christ and the glory of God.

---

[41] Colossians 1:28

Whoa, right? I mean, if *that* is the perfect marriage then let's just settle for barely scraping by the lofty standard. Far too many marriages end in divorce, so if we can just set the bar at 'mediocre', trying just to keep the thing on the rails then we're doing all right. I feel that way. Really. In most of these topics of perfect *this* or perfect *that* there is a sense of intimidation and impossibility. Some of them are laughable at times. These expectations seem extraordinarily difficult when our relationships are going well, so if we start coming apart at the seams they feel like some kind of sick joke.

We must keep coming back to the motivation thing, though. What is it we *want*? No performance in marriage will be perfect. Husbands will screw up and forget to pick up the milk and bread, or maybe even a kid or two. Wives will frustrate and disappoint. Arguments will happen. Somebody will be on the other side of a silent treatment and somebody else will shout something they shouldn't. Are these performances admirable?

Nope. Are these the desire of either spouse? Now THAT is the question!

A perfect spouse is one who wants exactly what is right. Remember our orientation in this perfection concept. Something is perfect when it does what it is designed to do. In the same way, marriage is perfect when it does what it was designed to do. Spouses are perfect when they do what they were designed to do. And so, what is a spouse designed to do?

Marriage is a relationship designed to change us and assist in the sanctifying work of the Holy Spirit to our souls. Our love for our spouse teaches us about love. The arena of marriage becomes the ground on which sacrificial love is practiced, sexual love is purified, and holy love is magnified. Through the lessons of our marriages we are purified in Christ. Through the lessons of Christ we become better spouses.

Marriages often end or flounder with the words "I'm not happy anymore." In those words we see the inward bend of the heart, scraping away the giving nature of love itself. Marriage teaches us the shape of love with its force and hope, ending in another, the beloved. The perfect spouse gives love generously and receives love patiently. Therefore, happiness becomes a product of the marriage, not a purpose. Our spouses refine us by partnering with the Holy Spirit to carefully and diligently perfect us. While the work is painful we praise our beloveds, our spouse, and the Spirit, for the help they are to us. Only by their perfecting love are we taken deeper into the presence of the God we love most.

It takes small steps to arrive at perfection. I mean, maybe you just happened to marry someone who was heads and tails above the crowd. I hope you did. If you didn't (you probably didn't) then the work begins. Or maybe neither of you started the marriage out as flawless people without mistakes or problems. If you didn't (you totally didn't) then the work begins. Much of the last couple paragraphs certainly sound great, but the stretch toward that greatness can also make us nervous. Do we really trust our spouse to work with the Holy Spirit to "fix" us? Isn't that a big hairy step of audacious trust! Yep. It is. So let's take small steps *toward our goal.*

Usually the process of healing our marriages toward the beautiful refining fire of holiness begins with a season of repentance, forgiveness, and renewal. Even if you have been married for a day, the season might be shorter, but it's going to happen. It's just the way this sort of thing always goes. We need to take care of the past before we start marching into the future.

Let's not fake a dance and just rally behind an emotional moment to make things right. Even our *best* pretending will eventually fall apart. Instead, take some time to sit down, humble yourselves before each other and have some solid conversations about hurts, pains and grudges. Be sure there are no buried hatchets in the heart or hidden injuries that might thwart forward progress.

Let these conversations sound like grace and mercy with these kinds of questions:

1. *Have I done anything to hurt you that I haven't apologized for?*

2. *Do you sense anything in my love for you that seems impure or selfish?*

3. *Do you feel I prioritize you correctly? Are there things I am placing above you that shouldn't be there?*

4. *What can I do to help our love grow?*

The success of the conversation relies on two key ingredients. First, are both of you living in a sustaining relationship with God? If ongoing sin has not been repented of or if the relationship with God is broken all together then the conversation will be nearly impossible or severely limited. Second, are both of you interested more in the success of the other and the unity of the marriage, or are you mounting a personal defense and competitiveness toward 'winning' the chat? The goal, if we love, is to see our spouse 'win'. As trust is developed over time, we will be able to give ourselves to our spouses and help them win conversations, trusting that as we refuse to become defensive, they will not abuse us and take advantage of our vulnerability.

Once the process of healing old wounds has been given ample time to do its work, the marriage can move to a discussion about the future. Trust enables you to give yourself to your spouse. That trust, paired with an intimacy with God, enables you with a desire for your spouse to work in partnership with the Holy Spirit to refine your soul.

The perfect Christian wants to live a life that glorifies God. The perfect spouse wants the marriage to be a change agent, moving *both* parties toward a life that glorifies God. In both cases, the glory of God is the obsession of the heart. A perfect spouse wonders, "Is God glorified in our marriage?"

Christ's love for the Church offers us an example of marital love to admire and study. A

long time ago, St. John Chrysostom wrote
beautifully of this example:

> *He (Christ) did not make her
> (the Church) merely beautiful but also
> young, not according to the nature of
> her body, but according to the state of
> her character. And this is not the only
> marvel, that when He found her ugly,
> shameful and old he did not abhor her
> ugliness but handed Himself over to
> death and refashioned her in
> unimaginable beauty. It is even more
> marvelous that after this, when He
> often sees her soiled and spotted, He
> does not reject her, not cast her away
> from Himself, but continues to care
> for her and correct her.*[42]

Christ is the perfect spouse. As we are
filled with His love, we too will become perfect
in our marital love. We won't be perfect in our
behavior, conduct, or performance because the

---

[42] St. John Chrysostom, *On Marriage and Family Life*, (St.
Vladimir's Seminary Press, 1986)

perfect spouse is human. Perfection in a spouse is a comment on the heart, the intention, and the desire.

By God's design, the perfect spouse loves with His love, hopes with His will, helps with His compassion, hurts with His heart, and heals with His touch. If something is forgotten, the perfect spouse regrets the failure of the human mind and sorrows over the lost opportunity to express a burning love. If something is mistaken, the perfect spouse yearns to sooth the wound and places the benefit of the beloved in a place of prominence over the house. Celebration is common. Encouragement is natural. Love is lavishly given and gracefully received. The perfect spouse's mind desires to admit wrongs and commits itself to improvement. In the face of failure, the perfect spouse proceeds optimistically for humility is the backbone of Christian endurance.

We can all be perfect spouses. Don't allow the bar of excellent behavior to pummel your heart to pieces. One small step at a time, move together, toward Him, and progress will come. Patiently pursue a first love together in Christ and reap the reward: a perfected love for each other.

CHAPTER SEVEN

THE PERFECT PARENT

Discipline. Is that the first word that came to your mind? The chapter title is "perfect parent" and a bunch of us just thought "discipline". Why is that? Why is it that so much of our understanding about parenting is so concretely connected to the discipline methods and what works and what doesn't? The disciplining of our children is often like the second wave of newly wed arguments. That first year of marriage is rough. It takes some hard times and perseverance to get through the early adjustments. At just about the time we seem to get the waters leveled out, a new storm comes in the form of a growing first child. The baby looks beautiful and steals our hearts and we love it so much and then the crazy thing breaks a rule. Now what?

Well I think discipline is actually a good place to start in this chapter, even though it's not really the center of our answer. A perfect parent is not defined by their discipline methods. Rather, the disciplining of our children is a pointer to the perfection of our parenting. Remember again, perfection isn't a static achievement; it's a direction of the heart, a motivation. So in this case of parenting, the motivation of the discipline is the result of the perfection of the parent. Did you put the kid in the corner? I'm sure that could work but the question is "why did you choose that discipline". Did you make them write sentences? Send them to their room? Those could work fine but the question is "why".

I'm picking on the discipline thing first for two reasons. One: we almost always begin with discipline when talking about the struggles and successes of parenting. It's just easy to jump into the common thought process rather than try to rewrite the order and ask us all to gravitate somewhere else. Two: discipline is an easy-to-see marker that shows us a way into the heart. Often, our disciplining comes in a time of emotion toward a person with whom we have some history and in the midst of some sort of social pressure. There's a lot at stake.

So if we use discipline as our little trail to follow into the heart of the parent, what is our first breadcrumb? To identify the breadcrumbs going backwards we begin at the end result: the chosen punishment. It usually goes in this order: the punishment is the result of a decision we make, the decision is the result of our reaction to the broken rule, the broken rule is the decision of the child and the child is the result of the parent. Ouch. I don't like that last statement. I know it's pretty broad, maybe even more so than what is actually true. There are lots of influences on our children that aren't us. School. Community. Friends. Culture. These other voices have been pouncing on our helpless little ones since before they even knew how to speak back. As a parent, we want to take responsibility for the way our kids turn out but this statement, "the child is the result of the parent", well, that's a bit much.

No matter how you process that statement, you must admit that at the very foundation of parenting is a deep acceptance of responsibility for the child. We shutter at "result" because it sounds so full and complete. Even if we have accepted responsibility, we prefer to keep our distance from the weak areas of that little kid and encourage ourselves by putting the blame on something else, anything else, just not us.

Well if we are going to move forward then we have to make some sort of an agreement here. Good parents take responsibility for their children. Are we good with that statement? I'm not letting us off the hook for the "result" idea but at least this phrase says the same thing in a bit more palatable way. So, using our agreement, let's follow the discipline line in normal order. First, we take responsibility to raise our children and they are the result of our effort. Second, the child breaks a rule of some kind. Third, we react to the broken rule. Fourth, we make a decision based on our reaction. Lastly, we punish based on our decision. There are some small movements and thoughts among those steps but for the most part we see about five major things happening.

Okay, remember now, we are using this process to follow the steps into the heart of the parent. We're trying to find out what a perfect parent is. Let's go back to our definition: something is perfect when it does what it was designed to do. Therefore, a parent is perfect when they do what they were designed to do. And so what is a parent designed to do?

Do you know what the Shema is? It is a special prayer from Deuteronomy that became a major part of Jewish worship. You've heard it before probably but you might just not know it had a name. It goes like this: "*Listen, O Israel! The Lord our God, the Lord is one*." Those are the words of Deuteronomy 6:4. The next verse is hugely important too. Do you remember the couple of times in the Gospels when someone came to Jesus and asked what they were supposed to do if they wanted eternal life? The question comes in Luke 10 and Mark 12. In both cases the answer is a quote from Deuteronomy 6:5, "*And you must love the Lord your God with all your heart, all your soul, and all your strength.*" Those are the very words we referenced earlier in the book as we were trying to figure out what 'perfect' means. Wow! These are some strong passages back there in Deuteronomy! If we go back and look at them closely and keep reading, we will find some other good stuff. Here is Deuteronomy 6:6-9: "*And you must commit yourselves wholeheartedly to these commands that I am giving you today. Repeat them again and again to your children. Talk about them when you are at home and when you are on the road, when you are going to bed and when you are getting up. Tie them to your hands and wear them on your forehead as reminders. Write them on the doorposts of your house and on your gates."*

"Repeat them again and again to your children." That's our answer right there. What is a perfect Christian? A perfect Christian is someone who loves the Lord their God with all their heart, all their soul and all their strength. What is a perfect parent? A perfect parent is someone who loves the Lord their God with all their heart, all their soul and all their strength and teaches these things to their children again and again.

From here we're going to take a couple routes. First, we're going to solve the discipline puzzle we opened up earlier. Then, once we've got that hammered out we will tackle a couple other elements of parenting.

A perfect parent, living in pure love for God, will naturally have a related effect on the children. As the parent lives in love with God the children will be powerfully impacted by that example. The impact is only an influence though, not a certainty. Every person makes their own decisions so we can't say something

85

like "perfect parents raise children who are perfect Christians". People aren't robots. Even the best of parents will weep at the struggles and pains of their wayward children. In the discipline situation I brought up earlier, I outlined a process, a step-by-step path we take in discipline from broken rule to punishment. I suggested that following the path backward would take us into the heart and reveal whatever perfection might exist in the parent. Let's do that now.

Our process went in reverse as follows: the punishment is the result of a decision we make, the decision is a result of our reaction to a broken rule, the broken rule is a decision of the child and the child is a result of the parent. There are four elements here but let me highlight two of them. First, the decision is a result of our reaction to a broken rule. How does the perfect parent react? Boy, that's a loaded question. There's a ton of hidden explosives underneath but let's just walk straight in to it. One of those explosives is in our emotions.

Do we parent out of our emotions? Or better, because emotions aren't all bad, let's ask "is our parenting controlled by our emotions". When that moment comes that the decision is being made to punish for a broken rule, we can see into the heart of that parent by examining the motivation and the desired outcome. If the love of God has overwhelmed us then we view our children with His love. In that love, we do not respond to broken rules saying "they must pay" but instead saying "they must grow". God's love for us, being perfect in justice, is forward in its momentum. He doesn't hold grudges, stay bitter or seek revenge. The love of God is a progressive, optimistic, redeeming love that always considers the betterment of the soul using a lesson today for the progress of the person tomorrow. In every punishment of God toward mankind there was a plan and purpose for how that punishment would positively impact the future. Following His example and filled with His love we too discipline our children perfectly when we seek their best for tomorrow no matter how we feel today.

The emotions in our chests can feel like a freight train without brakes. Within the family our reactions are stirred to a boiling pitch because our investment in these people is deeper than anywhere else. They know what get's under our skin. They know exactly where the last straw is and sometimes they wave in front of our faces taunting us with an impending emotional collapse. How does the perfect parent deal with this ridiculous problem?

Parental perfection is the heart that breaks itself for the benefit of a child. The moment we see that babies face for the first time, the soft skin, the toes so tiny they can't be real; we're hooked. They make a babbling noise and we just about pass out from overwhelming joy. In those early moments of parenting we connect with our children and commit ourselves to them for the first time in the flesh. The apple of our eye has become the hand in our hand. And yet, one day we will watch will great sorrow as that hand defies us. The tiny toes walk away from us. The soft skin grows calloused against us. In some degree, while not always a monumental rebellion, all children disobey and cause division in the relationship. In the emotional response to that division it is the responsibility of the parent to sacrificially love the child with a willingness to be broken for the sake of healing. There is no room for pride here. Parental love is the death of pride and the absolute celebration of the soul of a child even at the expense of the self. Such is the Gospel.

We are the babies born of God into this world and lost to it through our disobedience to God Himself. The Father from which we were created was the very One we turned away from. Our hearts were calloused and filled with sin. In His emotional response, one of love and great fiery passion, He sacrificed of Himself. God in Christ "took the humble position[43]" and "died a criminal's death[44]". In

---

[43] Philippians 2:7
[44] Philippians 2:8

an expression of the love of God the Father for us, His children, He was broken for our healing. What greater example could we possibly require?

A perfect parent loves the Lord with heart, soul and strength and speaks of that love to the children again and again. How do we speak the love? We live it. Our love *for* God ends up filling us with the love *of* God. With a heart full of His love we parent, we punish, we reward and we guide.

In the times I've publically spoken of my parents I've made a couple statements I stand by. First, they weren't perfect. Second, they were perfect. Their perfection was not in performances of wisdom, punishment, guidance, entertainment and so on. Their perfection was in their desire, their love and the way they pointed me to a better Father, a better parent. I can list to you the ways my parents messed up. However, as I now reflect on the experiences of my childhood I see their heart. I saw it then but I was a child and I thought as a child. As a man, as a father now, I see more clearly how they parented. Not perfect, but perfect. They loved the Lord with everything they had and they told me about it again and again. His love filled them and guided them and I got to see it and touch it and know it. As I grew, I found myself rooted by His love because it was my normal.

We were talking about emotions and the backward discipline process from the beginning. The first one we grabbed ahold of was the emotional response to the broken rule. The other one, I haven't pointed it out yet, is the child as a "result of the parent". As the result of my parents I can see how the love of God in them is my strength today and the weaknesses of their humanity contributes to my weakness today. I am the result of them. The same thing is happening to my kids. I see how my wife and I love the Lord with everything we have and it changes my children. They are being formed by the love of God as it is alive in my wife and my self. Their strength is God's love through us. In the same way, their weakness is kind of our fault. We aren't perfect folks. Our low points seem to have become their low points. They have their own personalities and all but when we see the common threads between them we get a little queasy in the stomach. My wife and I chuckle uncomfortably at their exposed weakness and say, "Uh, that's you honey."

Who are you in your perfect parenting? Are you loud? Are you indecisive or emotional? Are you stoic and removed? Does your spouse have to constantly tell you to spend time with your children? Do you over-celebrate your little prince or princess? We all have these bent or weird problems in our personalities that impact our parental labors. We're human. However, we must believe that God's love in a person is powerful. If we love the Lord with everything we have and teach that love to our children again and again then we can taste the sweetness of perfect parenting.

A perfect parent sees the wedding of their newborn on the day of their birth and prays for a suitable partner. A perfect parent holds their child loosely in the hands making a constant surrender to God the Father. Pain is shared. Lessons are careful. Schedules and tasks are lived out together with victories and losses a family affair. The child's curious ideas are legitimized. Wrong is called wrong. Tomorrow is a bright new swing of the bat and the perfect parent stands with hand over hand at the plate. Encouragement is most concerned with the soul because outward beauty fades. Punishment is most concerned with growth because revenge isn't in the vocabulary. As the perfect parent struggles with personal weakness, every effort is made to strangle the problem and minimize generational cursing. Broken for the benefit of the child. Exhausted for the energizing of the child. Transparent for the wisdom of the child. A perfect parent loves the Lord with absolutely everything and says exactly that, again and again, to a generation consequently made better.

CHAPTER EIGHT

THE PERFECT CHURCH

We are the Church. I guess that's the short answer. The Church isn't a building it's a people. Paul wrote, "All of you together are Christ's body, and each of you is a part of it." He then went on to describe the different roles within the Church and how we can't all do the same thing. It's a lesson on cooperation and teamwork. At the end he wrote, "So you should earnestly desire the most helpful gifts. But now let me show you a way of life that is best of all." Then comes the amazing chapter on love that we use for every sermon, lesson, lecture and talk all the way up to the wedding its self: 1 Corinthians 13. Read how this awesome piece of Scripture opens up:

"If I could speak all the languages of earth and of angels, but didn't love others, I would only be a noisy gong or a clanging cymbal. If I had the gift of prophecy, and if I understood all of God's secret plans and possessed all knowledge, and if I had such faith that I could move mountains, but didn't love others, I would be nothing. If I gave everything I have to the poor and even sacrificed my body, I could boast about it; but if I didn't love others, I would have gained nothing."

Absolutely beautiful writing! If the Church is made up of Christian individuals and this statement, among others, described the individuals then shouldn't this also describe the Church as a whole? It should. It's not just a description of a single person. It's a description of a group, a society, the Church.

Paul is comparing the external behavior with the internal motivation. He is talking about perfection. The six actions he refers to cover a wide range: speaking, prophecy, divine knowledge, faith, generosity and sacrifice. Each of these six external actions is held against an example that is on the extreme end of the spectrum. He isn't just referring to an above average speaker but to a mouth that knows every language in the world *and* even the language of the angels! I laughed when I just wrote that. Come on now, Paul. A little crazy with the examples here, aren't we? But I know, he's just making a point. When we relate his point to the Church, its potent.

I can't tell you how often I hear a church graded highly because the pastor is a good preacher. The preaching tends to take center stage on the main event of the week. In that way, we've kind of organized the whole Church thing to balance itself on the strength of a weekly sermon. For some, the Christian religion boils down to thirty minutes or less. Paul speaks to us, defining the perfect Church and saying, in effect, "even if your preaching and teaching was international and broadcast to the angels, it would just be an annoying noise if you didn't love others".

The topic then moves to spiritual strengths like the gift of prophecy, divine knowledge and faith. Paul says that even if all of these were true and love was lacking then "I would be nothing". Again we come back to these things we look for in the perfect church. We might want the ideas and discernment of our church to be well known and influential. We might want to be a part of a church that makes big decisions by faith. These are great! Paul just reminds us that even if we are the best in each of these areas we still look to love as the necessary ingredient.

Maybe you want to be a part of a church that gives a ton of money to the poor and to missionaries and to local charities. Maybe you want to be a part of a church that sacrifices and willingly endures struggles for the benefit of the global Church and the Kingdom of God. These are excellent attributes! And Paul writes, "I could boast about it; but if I didn't love others, I would have gained nothing." Fascinating, isn't it? The way we talk about a perfect Christian seems almost identical to the way we talk about the perfect Church.

I see two major moments in a person's life where the 'perfect church' conversation comes up. First, the person has just left a church or moved to a new city. In this case there is a need to find a new church. They consider factors like proximity to their house, style of worship, doctrine, leadership, friendliness of the people, etc. There are lots more but you get the point. These are typically the kind of things we look for in our search for the perfect church.

The second moment where a person might talk about the perfect church is an internal assessment. Most pastors do this at least once a week, probably more. Church leadership will have some sort of conversation related to this in each board meeting. Every member of a church has an ideal in mind and a view of reality for the church they attend. Periodically the ideal and the reality collide. We have a conflict between what we want and what we see. In a church of a hundred there are a hundred different 'wants', a hundred different ideal visions of a perfect church. To make it even more complicated, there are also a hundred different assessments of the church as it is right now. Everybody sees something different. Every once in a while these issues stir up wars in the pews over the color of the carpet and the church is torn in two. And for what? The perfect church.

I'm not trying to get too heavy or negative here. It's a painful truth. Our perception of the function of the Church, the expected benefits of the Church in our lives and the prioritization of those functions and benefits create a battlefield. Let me word that more simply.

We each see the church as designed for a certain purpose. Some see it as a place to be together. Some see it as a place to practice religion. Some see it as a community outreach center. There is truth to each of these but here's my point: every person has a different view of how their church should operate both publically (to the community) and personally (to me, I). My view or your view of the function/purpose isn't the same as the person sitting to our right or left. So it leaves us in a bit of an unspoken conflict, hoping that each person agrees with us.

The color of the carpet comment is a reference to a common fight. Actually, I don't know how common it really is. Somewhere along the way there has been more than one church body fight over what color the new carpet should be. In some of those cases the fight resulted in major rifts and even splits in the church. As a result, we use the 'color of the carpet' as a joking term to refer to silly fights in churches. Of course, the joke isn't funny. It's a result of imperfect people defining the church incorrectly. Only perfect people can make a perfect church. In other words, correctly motivated people make up the congregation of a correctly motivated church.

At the beginning of our definition of the perfect church we have to remove the human initiative. In other words, the Church isn't our idea. The believing community of the Church is the work of the Holy Spirit. We can come up with names, logos, building designs, sermon series ideas, children's programs and outreach missions but we can't come up with the Church. Without the work of the Holy Spirit, our gathering would be just that, a gathering, little more than a town hall meeting. By the anointing of the Holy Spirit our gathering of believers becomes a sacred place and sacred time where God uniquely interacts. It's not a human idea or a human work. This truth rests on a greater truth: any movement toward God begins in God. Even that tiniest startup energy of our first thought of worship is a product of God inserting His power into our lives. He is before.

Really, this is essential. Church planters have a ton of energy and endless ideas. Pastors lead with passion and believe in what they are doing. However, it isn't a human who starts a church. God the Holy Spirit, in an act of grace and love, makes possible the gathering of people to become an acceptable worship of God. The gathered people are then, by His work, called the Church.

Since it the Holy Spirit who brings about the Church, we know that it is a holy object. God, who is holy, will only bring about the purest of things, holy in their nature. God makes a holy Church out of people who are unholy but moving into holiness by His work. This doesn't mean that the Church is only as holy as the people in it. That would be like saying a hospital is only as clean as the patients in it. The Church is holy because it is God who makes it and keeps it. The perfect Church is designed by God to be holy, filled by God who is holy and kept holy by God. Those unholy persons who enter the Church are, by the function of the Church, to be made holy.

We've only solved half the problem so far. If you're looking from one church to another in an effort to find the 'perfect' one then there are some key indicators. What I've mentioned thus far is not an indicator but a prerequisite or precondition. The Holy Spirit is not the result of a church; the Holy Spirit is the cause of the Church. The existence of the Holy Spirit within a church comes before, as the basis on which the church began, not after, as the result of a churches effort. The Holy Spirit is predicating the church, not indicating. When we see the Holy Spirit active within a congregation we should be reminded that it was by His work they came to worship in the first place. His visible influence is the natural result of these believers obeying His idea to bring them together. The observable Holy Spirit power within a congregation is not some strange sign of a unique movement among the people. Rather, it is a natural occurrence of Church.

The perfect church is one that is brought about and held together by the Holy Spirit. The perfect church desires the glory of God above all things and the work of Christ to change all things by the power of the Holy Spirit in and through all things. God's perfection is to use the church as a change agent in the lives of people. He makes the unholy holy. Man's perfection is to love the Lord with everything (heart, mind, soul, strength) and love neighbor as self in a community of worship.

Is this even possible? Can this kind of a church exist? We've all seen how the church can mess up. The news covers stories from across the nation but chances are we have seen it right in our back yard, too. If you hang around long enough you might start thinking the Church is stuck, broken or even unfixable. The next logical thought is "What's the point?" It's not easy to speak of the problems in the Church in one breath and then discuss the reality of a perfect church in the next. Yet, it's just that, a reality. The perfect church is not something we float as a conversation starter or a childhood fantasy. It's not just the immature hope of an inexperienced young pastor. It's not just the overly optimistic outlook of the mega-church in the city. The perfect church can exist, should exist and does exist.

So you're driving around looking for that perfect church. You've understood that Holy Spirit is the starter and keeper, the holy purifying Pastor to us all. Now what? What are we looking for? While the Church begins in the supernatural, it is a physical natural object. It's made up of people we can see and hear. It's doing things we can watch and record and analyze. This divine idea now has observable traits. In the perfect church, what do these observable traits look like? Let's boil them down to three main areas[45].

First, the relationship with Jesus Christ is fundamental. This might seem obvious but it's not as common as it should be. Of course, Jesus is obvious, at least the mention of His name. The less obvious factors are the words 'relationship' and 'fundamental'. Both of these words are related to a previous chapter on the perfect Christian. Those loves, for God and

---

[45] These three concepts are adapted from Karl Barth's Dogmatics in Outline.

neighbor, are the result of a relationship with Jesus. Using His name in a song is not just a shout out or a pat on the back. The perfect Christian sees these as worshipful expressions of a real love to a real God. In the same way, the perfect church relates to God as a community in relationship with Jesus. In John 17 Jesus prayed to God the Father saying of us, "…that they may be one, just as We are one; I in them and You in me, that they may be perfected in unity"[46]. The individuals in the church are bonded together in agreement because their love for Christ is a unifying love. Worship is not just for singing. Preaching is not just for hearing. The Bible is not just for reading. The singing, hearing and reading activities in the perfect church are grounded in Christ and welded to His Work. The perfect church enjoys a fundamental community relationship with Christ.

Second, the call to missions is normal, not extra. I mentioned earlier in the book that I live in Africa. My family lives in Kampala,

[46] John 17:22-23

Uganda. Every few years we return to America to travel and fundraise and reconnect. There is something interesting that church folks often say to me. I'm not picking on any one church in particular. In fact, I would estimate that in probably 75% of the churches we visited at least one person said this: "We are a missions-minded church." It was usually said in a way that I think was supposed to bring me encouragement or comfort knowing that we missionaries would be taken care of. It could have meant other things, I suppose, but I could never quite figure it out. At first, I thought it was funny that every church was setting themselves apart by claiming the 'missions-minded' tag. Then I realized how strange the statement was. Missions-minded church? What does that mean? Is there such a thing as a church that *isn't* missions minded?

The perfect church, in relationship with Christ, considers missions as standard, normal and primary. It wouldn't be necessary for such a perfect church to claim the tag of being 'missions-minded' because, to them, and rightly so, missions and church are nearly synonymous. By it's very nature the Church is a public, social gathering of believers. It's from the calling of missionaries that the local church exists in the first place. Ambassadors of God do the work of God to bring up the Church of God that sends out the ambassadors of God. The system is pretty good.

If a perfect church is to speak about missions, the focus is not on whether it's being done but where and what way. Leaders in a perfect church don't treat 'sending' as an end goal but as the starting point. The perfect church considers the call to missions as normal, not extra.

Third, the kingdom of God is the unrivaled, unequivocal, unanimous destination. This is probably where most of us have lost sight of the perfect church in the fog and dust of battle. The spiritual war in human souls has stirred up behavior so disgusting we've questioned and wept over our pastors, our churches and maybe even our religion. Evil destroys. Sin has damaged our view of the

Church because we've likely always seen the church as a human invention. In the spiritual battles of our communities the church has always been, in our mind, the pastors attempt to persuade. Therefore, any fault or failure of the leader has been seen as a pointer to the hypocrisy of the message. "That pastor stands up there and says stuff he can't even live out himself!" It's a hard thing to fix but the perspective here is way off base.

If we are seeing the Church as a work of the Holy Spirit then we know it is not by human hands that it came together. The perfect church is not perfect in it's performance because it's full of people. My dad joked years ago, "This pastor job would be so much easier if it weren't for all the people." It's true! The worst part of the Church is the people in it. But, consider this: the sickest part of the hospital are the patients in it. However, if you remove the patients, what do you have? Certainly not a hospital. Remove the people and you have no church.

The perfect church is focused on the Kingdom of God as the destination. That destination is not just a stop at the end with no influence today. With the Kingdom of God as our destination, the movements of our broken community in the process of healing become a part of the work, not a distraction from it. We set our sights on purity and holiness trusting that God can and will do this in us. The Kingdom goal for tomorrow directs our hearts motivation for today. Barth wrote, "This goal of the Church is bound to constitute a continuous restlessness for the men in the Church, whose action stands in no relation to the greatness of this goal.[47]" When we see inconsistencies between belief and behavior we tend to struggle. It smells like hypocrisy. Sometimes it is. Other times it's the stench of sick people in the midst of their treatment. And at the moment we point a finger to call their stench "rotten" we should consider that our healing process might not smell too pleasant either.

---

[47] Karl Barth, *Dogmatics in Outline*, (Harper Torchbooks, 1959)

The perfect church is one motivated in the direction of the Kingdom of God. As such, it will fill itself with the sick and do it's best to bring healing. Even while sickness is seen, sickness is not the end goal. The sick (sinners) are accepted but not left untreated. Sinners are loved. In fact, they are loved so much that they are not left comfortable in their sin. The perfect church loves the sin right out of people.

So if you are either hunting for a perfect church or working within your local church to bring about perfection, here are just a few ideas for guiding questions to consider:

1. *Is Jesus the fundamental focus of relationships both on a personal level and at a social level?*
2. *Is missions a normal part of this church or is it at the exceptional edge? In other words, if missions is a luxurious extra then there is a problem.*
3. *Is the effort and eyesight of the church focused on the Kingdom of God as the destination?*

Notice that this chapter has not mentioned anything about style of music, doctrinal positions or what kind of people currently attend. There are all kinds of things to consider in choosing or leading a church. Much of what is elevated to the top of the priority list is actually nothing more than preference. The church that hits all the right notes on our list of preferences could be quite off base in the more important 'perfect' areas. Also, it's a good idea for us to spend more time asking, "Am *I* a perfect Christian?" rather than "Is *this* a perfect church?" Revival begins when someone says, "Let it begin in me!" Whatever we believe about the Church should first be true about us, personally, individually.

As you involve yourself in a local church I encourage you to join as a perfect Christian and do your part to bring perfection to your church. No church will perform perfectly but every church can be perfect.

CHAPTER NINE

THE PERFECT JOB

For about a year I worked as a 'personal assistant' with a home of mentally handicapped people. Most of that time was third shift. I helped them with supper, going to bed, getting up and eating breakfast. I learned a lot but I had no interest in making a career out of it. It was just something to pay the bills. After that job I worked in a casework factory. Casework is office cabinetry and countertops and reception desks, that sort of thing. I ran a big router machine that followed instructions from a computer. That job was second shift. Some days I really enjoyed it, others, not so much. But it wasn't a career either. It paid okay and it was secure so I stayed around until something better came along. Finally I got a job at a local university working in the accounting department. It was the career position I'd been looking for. I got to dress up a little and look nice at work. I got a desk of my own. It was 8-5 everyday with benefits. My wife and I were happy. It was the perfect job until it wasn't.

At that time in my life I was looking at the same things most of us look at. What does it pay? Does it have benefits? Is there room to move up? These priorities guided my decision making in how I assessed my occupational happiness. If the pay was too low, look for something else. If there was no room to move up, put in an application in greener pastures. Whatever position I had was judged by what it did for me. I graded the job based on how it made me feel, what it let me do and what privileges and luxuries it afforded me. In this way I think I was pretty normal. These are the common ways most of us think about our jobs. Don't get me wrong; there's nothing bad about wanting good pay, good benefits, etc. I think the real issue is with that word 'perfect' when we apply it to any area of life, in this case, a job.

For me, this problem of finding the 'perfect' job resurfaced when God called me to something new. Interestingly, His call did not begin with a direction but with a detachment. Before God gave me instructions for where to go He began reworking my heart to disconnect me from where I was. I think God does this kind of thing more than we recognize. Sometimes it feels like His instructions blindside us but I've wondered if He actually does things we so subtly and softly we don't ever see them. As big as the idea is now, maybe it would be even bigger had He not been working behind the scenes? I don't know. But I'm sure that in this case, He was helping me to obey before He ever gave me an instruction. As I started growing uncomfortable in that job I had loved, new thoughts and ideas were discovered swimming around in my head. I rejected them because I thought they were my own and I didn't want to distract myself from the task at hand. They increased. I actually got discouraged after a while because these unwanted thoughts began to really change how I felt about my job; the one I thought was perfect. It was July in a church service when I prayed and asked God what He had to say to me. In that moment He called me out of my job and into a fulltime formal ministry position. As I sit here today, a fulltime missionary, I can't imagine doing anything else. But I still wonder: what is the perfect job? If I thought I had it then and it changed then how can I be sure it won't change again?

I might sound a little silly in the way I'm talking about this. I'd be taking a different route entirely if I weren't so sure this is hitting an important note in our culture. One of the most common phrases referring to something 'perfect' is the 'perfect job'. It's the reason we go to school. It's the reason we work hard and hope for a promotion. It's the reason we build ourselves up so high on the resume. We all want that perfect job.

My story shows how the perfect job can change over time. There are thousands, millions of stories like mine. I think for many of us, the perfect job is elusive and possibly not even real. There are some who have noticed that the perfect job is just whatever job they don't have right now. They imagine: "Every job is perfect except mine!" The grass is always *perfecter*. And someday we will get the most *perfecterest* job ever! Right?

If we take a strong step of putting our cultural norms on hold and changing our angle of view on this 'perfect job' thing, what will we see? Have we made ourselves miserable with a wrong focus on occupation in the Christian life? Have we even wasted our time and energy working ourselves to the bone for…what? Where has the business ladder taken us? Sometimes these questions come to our mind when the professional world lets us down. Sometimes they come when the Holy Spirit speaks to us about our work. I believe they are the kind of questions that indicate a turning of the heart in the right direction.

The truth is: there is no job on the planet that is always the most fun, favorite, ideal position forever. In that way, the perfect job doesn't exist. Once you have it, you don't have it. That's because the perfect job isn't about the job at all but about human desire. When we refer to our 'perfect' position we are actually commenting on ourselves. A persons ideals in life disclose who they are, deep inside. A person swallowed up in greed finds the perfect job in any position that cuts a big check. A person who strives for power finds the perfect job anywhere they get to call the shots.

So if a person is a perfect Christian, as we've discussed in this book so far, then we know their deep insides have changed. They are pure in motive and focused solely on Jesus Christ and bringing glory to God. If that's the case, then what would a perfect Christian want in a perfect job? It would be defined quite differently, wouldn't it?

The perfect job, in the Christian sense of the phrase, is the work God has for us. The purpose of the position shifts from being a resource to being a tool. To the perfect Christian, a job isn't just something to do to pay the bills and make money and move up in life. All work is Kingdom work. All jobs are ministry positions. Every posting in life is a missionary posting. In that way, we're all pastors and missionaries because we are guiding others to Christ and reaching deep into the corners of our communities.

A previous pastor at our local church in Indiana spoke on this topic several years ago. To drive the point home, he walked through the isles of the congregation. He would pause and place his hand on the shoulder of someone saying, "You sir, you are a soldier of God cleverly disguised as a 3rd grade teacher." He moved to the next isle, "You ma'am, you are a soldier of God cleverly disguised as a store manager." He continued like this for a while. At first it felt like an illustration to drive a point home. Then, as he kept going and going, we realized he was not teaching, he was commissioning. These words can seem quite light and silly if we've heard them before. They come across as some cheap spiritual way of making the average working classes feel like they are a part of things. Well, it feels that way because it *is* that way. The working class, average American has just as much responsibility in ministry as the pastor and the missionary. The same is true of white-collar doctors, lawyers and architects. Every job is missions.

The perfect job is every job that God puts us in. It's not perfect by what it does for us but by what we do through it. Our jobs are not for selfish gain. God gives each of us an assignment and expects us to make the very most out of the work in front of us. Sometimes it is easy to see how our contribution benefits the Kingdom, other times it seems impossible that we are helping God with anything at all.

When I worked at the cabinet factory I would have a stack of two or three hundred panels that I was supposed to turn into doors with my machine. For hours I would do the same thing over and over again. During that monotonous work I thought about how little I was doing to spread the Gospel and bring God glory. I became bitter very quickly and felt like my time was just a complete waste. When comments came at church about this whole, "Nathan you are a soldier of God cleverly disguised as..." I wanted to throw up. I felt guilty for not being a good Christian. I felt intimidated by anyone doing more admirable Christian labor. It took time for me to develop a healthier view.

The perfect job is characterized in the same way no matter what the occupational title or company clout or references or pay or seniority. The perfect job is any work done for the glory of God. This work is dedicated to Him so that the benefits of the effort are added to His storehouse. The perfect worker submits all resources, expertise, talent and usefulness to the work of the Kingdom of God. This is not a blind donation to the Church but a wholehearted offering of a life to God. The tithe is only a monetized outpouring of a generous heart. The perfect Christian doesn't just give ten percent of the paycheck but 100% of the very life, blood, sweat and tears. The perfect job is a way of bleeding and sweating and crying the Gospel into this world. Evangelism doesn't happen without Christians exhausting themselves, giving every ounce, pouring every drop they have in a persistent obedience to our cause. The perfect job is toward the salvation of the world even if it comes in the form of a desk with a parking space, a tie, a promotion and the periodic casual Friday. These workplace things threaten to steal our attention and become the focus of our whole lives. Millions have been forgotten in their success and left nothing but a few bucks and an heirloom or two. Millions. But it doesn't have to be that way.

An older woman once came up to my wife, Jade, with a promise to contribute $100 a month to our ministry in Uganda. Jade replied in disbelief, "This is a lot of money!" The woman replied, "I'm going on a mission trip soon, too! I haven't got many years left but I want to finish tired and broke." We were struck by the woman's focus. Her whole life was purposed for the benefit of the Kingdom, the spreading of the Gospel.

I have a friend who has done very well in business. As a business owner he has experienced great financial success and professional success. However, he's frugal and purposeful with what he's been given. He lives in a modest home and he is one of the most charitable, helpful people I know. If you ask him why he lives the way he lives he will tell you about Jesus. This man is not looking for paychecks and ladders and benefits. He is obsessed with the Gospel. In his Christian perfection he loves the Lord with everything he has and his whole life is spent basking in it and sharing it. For that reason, he will always have the perfect job.

This perfection of life is gorgeous and freeing. The perfect job is a natural result of living the perfect Christian life. When the motivation of the heart is bent inward then all other areas of life follow suit. If love becomes something to make me happy rather than something I give then the marriage will struggle. If performance means everything to me then parenting will struggle. Like every other area of life, the perfect job is a result of an outward aiming heart, focused on Christ and fascinated with His majesty. When the eyes of our souls are captured in the radiance of his glory the hands and feet are energized to obedient participation in the work of the Kingdom.

CHAPTER TEN

THE PERFECT ENDING

I'll admit it's been fun writing a book where every chapter is a 'perfect' chapter. Even the book itself, I mean, this is perfect. Awesome. Aaaaaand fade to black.

What makes an ending perfect? I've seen some movies finish with such brilliance it seems like the whole world changed. The specific movie isn't coming to mind at the moment but I remember seeing one a while back in the theatre. When it finished, the audience (all strangers) just sat there for a while in astonishment. It was probably only a few seconds but it was a weird few seconds. A couple people clapped. Someone behind me said "whoa". The ending of that movie was breathtaking.

Some of my favorite books end that way, just perfect. It's such a right way of finishing the book that it becomes the focus of the whole thing as if the book was only written for the ending. One of my favorite authors, Fyodor Dostoevsky, wrote The Brothers Karamozov, one of the most famous pieces of literature ever written. It's a big brick shaped book so don't try it unless you have some time on your hands. Anyway, it ends with this perfect climactic and summarizing finish:

"And eternally so, all our lives hand in hand! Hurrah for Karamozov!" Kolya cried once more ecstatically, and once more all the boys joined in his exclamation."

Isn't that great? It captures this moment that never ends. The world of the story just keeps going. It puts a cap on the whole thing and sets the way the reader remembers the story. No matter what happens in the book, we know it ends with eternal friendship and cheering. So good.

I read another book recently called A Farewell To Arms. It's a Hemingway. I'd never read Hemingway, I don't think, maybe I did in highschool. It's a little dark. Not entirely clean. Hemingway wrote the book to describe war. As a soldier himself, he wanted to paint war with correct colors, making it in to the violent and awful thing it is. His last scene in the book is a perfect summary that leaves the reader in the bewildering realm the author has created. His perfect ending resolves to this sentence:

"After a while I went out
and left the hospital
and walked back to the hotel
in the rain."

Dark. That mental picture of a man leaving a hospital and walking away in the rain is what Hemingway wants the reader to feel. It's his perfect ending.

These endings are so powerful when they work. If something ends well it takes on a whole new level of appreciation. It leaves a residue of fascination in the brain and requires that we share it with others. We say, "Oh, I just finished (watching, reading, listening to) this whatever…you HAVE to check it out!" It's not that the beginning and middle weren't good or even great. It's just, wow, that ending. The ending just sealed the deal. Unless it wasn't good.

A bad ending is powerful too. Anytime there is some big television series that announces an end to the show there is a build up to the series finale. If it's good then all the diehard fans breathe a sigh of relief. If it's bad then CNN covers it like a national tragedy.

In the Christian perfection conversation, this perfect ending applies to several different ideas: retirement, death, legacy, etc. There are quite a few big themes that we put our heart and soul into for years, all of them connected to our endings. We talk about finishing strong but that's a fairly subjective term. We talk about our desire to hear God say the famous "well done good and faithful servant[48]" but is it just a desire for congratulations or is it a call to action? I guess my question is not just about defining the perfect ending but identifying how that perfect ending changes us today. After all, we don't really get to choose how we die or what people say about us once the book is closed. Even our retirement is a monster we have little control over.

I told you in the last chapter about that woman who wanted to finish life tired and broke. She has an inspiring perspective, to say the least. It's a pretty awesome ending, giving everything to the cause and finishing life with empty hands. We can all see the honor in her words. But are her words a definition of the

---

[48] Matthew 5:21

perfect ending? How does the perfect Christian finish?

So far we have covered the different major roles we play in life from spouse to parent to church-member to employee, we've covered all the bases. As we live this life in pure love of God with right motivation to His will, how then should we think of the ending?

It might seem like a good idea to separate each individual component of the "ending" and discuss each one with a subchapter on retirement, death, etc. However, in that case, each subchapter would just be a copy and paste of the previous. The perfection we have identified in this book is all about motivation and desire. Regardless of the angle we take on endings, the motivations are all the same. Actually, this principle truth can be applied everywhere. This book has specified a few images of the human life to discuss the Christian perfection we seek. However, the point has not been to create a comprehensive "how-to" on living. The point has been to use these life circumstances to develop angles and colors giving a crystal clear image of perfection in the Biblical sense. As such, we can take those clear images and examine any other areas of interest. It's not a new teaching, it's Biblical. It's holiness as old as time itself. In that way, it has no beginning and ending for it originates and exists within God. The perfection we discuss is not a human effort or exertion. Only God is perfect. Whatever perfection is found in us comes from the Holy Spirit within us, energizing our purely motivated hearts toward Him. God is our perfection.

The perfect ending is God. Not that God is an end because God does not end. Rather, God is *our* end. We end in Him just as we began in Him. The perfect Christian lives every breath for the glory of God even to the end of life itself. From this powerful position we get martyrs, those individuals who lived their lives for the glory of God even to the very threat and completion of their death. Perfect living brought them death, the perfect ending. I know that sounds pretty dark too but it's not. It's bright. Not that all death is the perfect ending.

I didn't say that. I'm saying that any time a thing ends for the glory of God then it ends perfectly.

There's nothing wrong with retirement unless the purpose is inwardly focused. There's nothing wrong with legacy unless the building of it is an inwardly focused effort. These endings in life are scattered and varied in degree. We end jobs. We move to new cities and end relationships. We end phases of life. We end habits. Things come and go. To the perfect Christian, they come and go for good reasons. Not just good, holy. Endings are glorifying milestones shouting praise of the Lord from their fixed position in time.

In this way, we have very limited control over how, when or why things end. We don't just get tired of things in life and wander off quietly. We don't just stomp out in anger because things aren't going the way we hoped or demanded. With God as our Lord, we've surrendered everything unto Him. He gets to make these decisions. He gets to say "stop" and "go" and we celebrate His wisdom and glorify Him through our happy obedience. The perfect

Christian begins and ends things often in ways that have no human wisdom in mind. The purpose is not to only do things in a way that makes the most sense (to a human) but to follow the will of God in His timing, direction and pace. In fact, the will of God instructs the timing such that the capabilities of the human, the amount of life left or whatever other "things to consider" are set on the curb. They matter, but only for a moment. Only long enough to be set back down in worshipful surrender.

My grandmother went overseas late in life to do missionary work in the Czech Republic. Our whole family was shocked when she first told us about her plans. Grandpa had passed away a few years before, and she was living by herself. Rather than closing up shop and settling into an easy routine, she packed up her things and went to work. We were inspired. She had set a bar for the whole family, that the work of the Kingdom of God is worth every day, every penny.

I've watched others behave this way too. An older couple showed up at a missionary training that was filled with families like ours, all 20's and 30's. They were in their late 60's and heading to join ministries and get work done. It was their perfect ending. I admire those who left something in their prime saying, "It's time. God is moving us." The perfect ending is the result of obedience to God. It comes when a person closely follows His will and moves in and out of life's circumstances by His hand. King David wasn't always a king. He refused to bring an end to King Saul even though Saul tried to kill him and God had chosen David to be the replacement. It would make sense for David to defend himself by killing Saul and taking the throne. David refused saying, "(Saul) is the Lord's anointed"[49]. The perfect ending was to let Saul live even though it made little sense to human logic.

When perfect Christians think about endings they do not think first of themselves. The ending is the song of story, the final capstone, the summary of the message. If the message of our lives is the glory of God then the

---

[49] 1 Samuel 24:10

endings we experience will follow that very plotline. We end selflessly and we are ended selflessly. By pure, holy love we begin and end all things, big and small, with a heart motivated to serve and glorify God.

As Jesus accepted His ending with a statement of accomplishment, we follow His example by giving our whole lives toward a final breath of glory to God saying, "It is finished"[50].

---

[50] John 19:30

Search me, O God, and know my heart;

test me and know my anxious thoughts.

Point out anything in me that offends you,

And lead me along the path of everlasting life.

Psalm 139:23-24

140

DISCUSSION QUESTIONS FOR
SMALL GROUPS

THE PERFECT PROBLEM

GROUP DISCUSSION QUESTIONS

Before we get into first chapter stuff, let's talk about why we are here…

1. What have you heard about this book?

2. Why did you decide to join this group and study this book?

3. What do you hope to get out of this time?

Okay, now on to the first chapter…

1. Nathan referred to the first time he ever heard words like "holiness", "sanctification" and "Christian perfection". Have you heard those words before? If so, when and where did you first hear them? How did they make you feel?

2. We all have a different story. Nathan shared about his upbringing and how his past impacted his view of Christianity. Take some time to go around the room and share your stories. Don't rush! This part is important!

3. Think about this Chapter 1 quote: *"The burden of perfect living stretches through the whole of our American history and culture, impacting the way we set our goals, parent our children, and reflect on the value of the life we have lived."* What areas in your life do you feel the most pressure to perform "perfectly"? Why?

4. Here's another quote to think through: *"We measure ourselves against the people around us and look for ways to feel good about our Christianity. In this way, holiness becomes a contest of churchy behavior."* Has this been your experience?

5. Here's James 1:2-4: *"Dear brothers and sisters, when troubles of any kind come your way, consider it an opportunity for great joy. For you know that when your faith is tested, your endurance has a chance to grow. So let it grow, for when your endurance is fully developed, you will be perfect and complete, needing nothing."* How do these verses make you feel? How do they relate to what you have thought a "perfect Christian" was?

● ● ● ● ●

CHAPTER TWO

GETTING IT RIGHT

1. The church in Africa wanted the holiness preaching to "relax". Have you ever felt that way about holiness preaching? How do people typically respond to holiness teaching in our churches today?

2. Nathan wrote: *"Here's the truth: nothing is lighter on the human spirit than holiness."* Has that been your experience? Share your feelings about this statement on holiness and how it relates to your personal experience.

3. Share what you think about this statement on holiness: *"We don't make it, we receive it. We do not create holiness anywhere, especially not in ourselves."* Do you think most people live this way? What's the difference between receiving holiness and trying to create holiness in ourselves?

4. What was the new definition of "perfection" from the story about Kevin

sanding the wood project? Is it the same as what you have understood in the past? If not, how is it different?

5. Nathan quoted Paul's words from Galatians 3:3 *"Are you so foolish? Having begun by the Spirit, are you now being perfected by the flesh?"* Can you think of a place in your life where you tend to turn to your own strength and capabilities rather than working in partnership with God, leaning into the power and love of the Holy Spirit?

6. The goal of this chapter is to get it right. Did we reach our goal? Do you feel like you have a better grasp on the topic with a healthy definition of perfection and holiness? If not, share your thoughts with the group and see how you might work together to fill in the gaps.

● ● ● ● ●

CHAPTER THREE

JOHN & CHARLES

1. Had you heard of John and Charles Wesley before reading this chapter? Did this brief history help you? What did you like about it?

2. Think about Wesley's statement that the perfect Christian is *"sanctified throughout, even to have a heart so all-flaming with the love of God as continually to offer up every thought, word and work as a spiritual sacrifice, acceptable to God through Christ. In every thought of our hearts, in every word of our tongues, in every work of our hands, to show forth his praise, who hath called us out of darkness into His marvelous light."* How do you feel about that? What thoughts and emotions are stirred up?

3. Wesley expressed a concern over those who might teach behaviors without teaching the reason behind the behavior. Eventually, legalism is born from this

error. What has been your history with legalism?

4. Even after Nathan thought about Christian perfection through the ideas of Wesley, the teaching of the Bible and his personal experiences with legalistic holiness, he still said, *"As intimidating as it is, even with the pain it's caused, I'm attracted to it."* Do you agree with him? What attracts you to it? What repels you?

5. We covered the Wesleyan background and looked at how our history has shaped us today. What other key figures, events, ideas or elements in your history have impacted your ideas about holiness and perfection?

● ● ● ● ●

CHAPTER FOUR

WHAT I BELIEVE
GROUP DISCUSSION QUESTIONS

1. What did you think about George and his path to Christian perfection? What did you learn from the story?

2. Let's try a vocab test! Can you define these words?
   a. Conviction
   b. Justification
   c. Regeneration
   d. Sanctification

3. How does your story line up with George's? You may not have experienced the events in the same order or manner. Can you testify from your story about your own experience with each of these things that George encountered?

4. Nathan wrote, "perfect ain't always perfect". What did he mean by that? Has that been your experience?

5. One of the words left off of our vocab test was "perfection". Think about the example of Kevin's wood project from chapter two, the history lesson and the example from George. Can you define the word "perfection"?

* This concludes the first part of the book. In the first four chapters, Nathan set out to identify the problem, look at the history behind it and suggest healthy solutions. Before moving on to the final six chapters, it might be good to take a moment for review and share some meaningful thoughts, challenges or quotes from the book thus far.

● ● ● ● ●

CHAPTER FIVE

THE PERFECT CHRISTIAN

1. Did this chapter change your view of the term "perfect Christian"? In what way was it changed?

2. Nathan shared a little bit about his salvation experience. What's your story? How did you remember your salvation?

3. What did you think about the "try for a B" problem? Have you noticed certain areas where you work hard to get a good grade? How does that "earning" attitude make you feel?

4. Much time was spent in this chapter pointing at the heart with words like motivation, intention and desire. Do you ever notice a gap between your desire and your action? In other words, do you identify with Paul who admitted in Romans 7:15, *"I don't really understand myself, for I want to do what is right, but I don't do it. Instead, I do what I hate."*

5. When you think about God being concerned more with your motivations than your behaviors, what do you feel? Is it helpful to think about God viewing you in that way?

6. We say, "even perfect Christians make mistakes". Some critics might disagree with our position. How would you respond to someone who says that all this focus on motivation and purity of intention is an excuse to behave however you want?

● ● ● ● ●

CHAPTER SIX

THE PERFECT SPOUSE

1. Do you remember what you felt before you started this chapter? When you saw that it was called "the perfect spouse", what did you think?

2. Now that you have finished the chapter, how do your thoughts about the perfect spouse differ? How are they the same?

3. Nathan wrote, *"If we love our spouses perfectly, we will love them into the arms of Christ before our own."* What do you think about that? How does that play out in the day-to-day routines of life?

4. Here's another quote: *"The arena of marriage becomes the ground on which sacrificial love is practiced, sexual love is purified, and holy love is magnified."* What are some other elements of the Christian life that can be "practiced" in the marriage arena?

5. Have you heard the "I'm not happy

anymore" statement about a marriage? Compare how you felt about it then versus how you might feel about it now.

6. For those who are married: Nathan explained how marriage is a tool that God uses to "fix" us. Perhaps you would like to share some reflections on ways that God has worked in partnership with your spouse to do a little repair work, updates or improvements.

7. There were four questions suggested to help set the stage for some good growth. Can you think of any other good questions that might be helpful?

8. Nathan wrote, *"humility is the backbone of Christian endurance"*. What do you think he meant by that? How does it apply to our marriages?

● ● ● ● ●

CHAPTER SEVEN

THE PERFECT PARENT

1. Same drill as chapter six: What did you think about the chapter title? Before you started reading, when you saw those words "the perfect parent", what did you think?

2. Do you feel you are fairly good at disciplining your children? Why are you good/not good?

3. Based on your understanding of the chapter, how would you answer this question: *"What is the purpose of a parent?"*

4. Someone in the group volunteer to read that passage from Deuteronomy 6:6-9: *"And you must commit yourselves wholeheartedly to these commands that I am giving you today. Repeat them again and again to your children. Talk about them when you are at home and when you are on the road, when you are going to bed and when you are getting up. Tie them to*

your hands and wear them on your forehead as reminders. Write them on the doorposts of your house and on your gates." What are your reactions to that text? Is this verse happening today?

5. We don't respond to our children's failures saying *"they must pay"* but instead *"they must grow"*. Discuss what this approach might look like. What does this approach demand of us as parents?

6. What are some things God has shown in his "parenting" of you that changed (or should change) the way you parent your own children?

● ● ● ● ●

CHAPTER EIGHT
THE PERFECT CHURCH
GROUP DISCUSSION QUESTIONS

1. What is the greatest strength of the church you currently attend?

2. What were the original factors that caused you to choose to attend your current church?

3. In his emphasis on the role of the Holy Spirit, Nathan taught, *"We can come up with names, logos, building designs, sermon series ideas, children's programs and outreach missions but we can't come up with the Church."* Without pointing fingers or naming names, what are the places in your church where you are most likely to rely more on human effort and expertise than Holy Spirit wisdom and guidance?

4. If a perfect church is meant to bring people to health then sick people must be welcomed. Is sickness permitted in your church? How could your relationship to the sick and hurting improve?

5. The first thing we look for in a perfect church: the relationship with Christ is fundamental. What might a church look like if the relationship with Jesus Christ were *not* fundamental? What kinds of things typically take His place?

6. The second thing we look for in a perfect church: missions is normal. What might a church look like if missions were *not* normal, but the extravagant special luxury? What might that church care about instead?

7. The third thing we look for in a perfect church: the Kingdom of God is the destination. What might a church look like if the Kingdom of God were *not* the destination? What other wrong destinations could there be?

8. The best way to be in a perfect church is to be a perfect Christian working within the church community. In what ways can you best improve your contribution to the church community?

CHAPTER NINE

THE PERFECT JOB

GROUP DISCUSSION QUESTIONS

1. After reading this chapter, do you think that we have to "like" every job we have? Is "liking" a job important? Is "liking" a job everything?

2. Nathan said in the past he graded his job based on how it made him feel, what it let him do and what privileges and luxuries it afforded him. Is that how you have graded your jobs? What are some other factors you may have considered when looking for a job?

3. Do you agree that *"all jobs are missionary postings"*? Is it true of your job? Why is it difficult for some to view their occupations as missionary work?

4. If *"all jobs are missionary postings"* then shouldn't they all have similar job descriptions? What kinds of things do Christians do in their jobs no matter what

job they have? When thinking of Christians in the work place, what are the common responsibilities on all job descriptions regardless of the occupation, pay, hours or status?

5. What are some changes you need to make to your current job in order to make it a "perfect" job?

6. It would be so great to end this discussion with some stories about times when your jobs have been "perfect". Tell your group about a memorable time when you were able to use your job for Kingdom work.

●　●　●　●　●

CHAPTER TEN

THE PERFECT ENDING

1. There are many different uses of the word "ending". The chapter referred to several including retirement, death, legacy and major life changes. What topic did you gravitate towards as you read? What kind of ending is on your mind right now? Why?

2. What is the impact of a bad ending?

3. What is the impact of a good ending?

4. Nathan wrote, *"any time a thing ends for the glory of God then it ends perfectly"*. Sometimes this idea is a tough pill to swallow. Perhaps you've had something end suddenly or painfully. What are some examples of situations where a "perfect ending" is especially difficult?

5. In the chapter, Nathan explained how we do not get to just say "stop" and "go" whenever we want. God chooses our

beginnings and endings. We obey with *"happy obedience"*. What is *happy* obedience? Are there other kinds of obedience besides "happy"? How does happy obedience bring about a perfect ending?

6. What did Jesus mean when he said *"it is finished"*? Can we speak like that? What do we need to do in order to say *"it is finished"*?

● ● ● ● ●

References

Barth, Karl. Dogmatics in Outline. New York: Harper and Brothers, 1959.

Chrysostom, St. John. On Marriage and Family Life. Trans. Catherine P. Roth and David Anderson. Crestwood: St Vladimir's Seminary Press, 1986.

Collins, Kenneth. The Scripture Way of Salvation. Nashville: Abingdon Press, 1997.

Eckhart, Miester. Selected Writings. Trans. Oliver Davies. London: Penguin UK, 1994.

Haines, Lee M and Paul William Thomas. An Outline History of The Wesleyan Church. Sixth Revised. Indianapolis: Wesleyan Publishing House, 2005.

Oswalt, Dr. John. Called to Be Holy. Nappanee: Francis Asbury Press, 1999.

Peters, John L. Christian Perfection and American Methodism. New York: Abingdon Press, 1956.

W. T. Purkiser, Ph.D. The Biblical Foundations: Exploring Christian Holiness. Vol. 1. Kansas City: Beacon Hill Press, 1983. 3 vols.

Wesley, John. A Plain Account of Christian Perfection. Kansas City: Beacon Hill Press of Kansas City, 1966.

Wood, J.A. Perfect Love. Kansas City: Beacon Hill Press, 1912.

52681010R00097

Made in the USA
Middletown, DE
21 November 2017